Mastering Parenthood: Secrets to Being Great Parents

Pille Pat Du

Published by Pille Pat Du, 2024.

MASTERING PARENTHOOD: SECRETS TO BEING GREAT PARENTS

First edition. April 2, 2024.

ISBN: 979-8224713042

Written by Pille Pat Du.

Table of Contents

Chapter 1: The Journey of Parenthood 1

Chapter 2: Communication in Parenting...7

Chapter 3: Building a Strong Parent-Child Relationship 13

Chapter 4: Discipline and Guidance 18

Chapter 5: Nurturing Emotional Intelligence.................................... 23

Chapter 6: Encouraging Independence 28

Chapter 7: Handling Challenges and Conflict 33

Chapter 8: Supporting Your Child's Education 39

Chapter 9: Creating a Healthy Lifestyle 44

Chapter 10: Celebrating Parenting... 49

Chapter 11: Navigating Parenting Styles 54

Chapter 12: Balancing Work and Family Life................................... 60

Chapter 13: Sibling Relationships 65

Chapter 14: Technology and Parenting.. 71

Chapter 15: Single Parenting 76

Chapter 16: Blended Families.. 82

Chapter 17: Parenting Through Different Stages 87

Chapter 18: Parenting for the Future 92

Chapter 19: Practicing Self-Reflection and Growth 98

Chapter 20: Conclusion..103

Chapter 1: The Journey of Parenthood

- Understanding the Responsibilities of Parenthood

Parenting is a profound and life-altering experience that comes with a wide range of responsibilities. From providing love and support to ensuring the physical, emotional, and educational well-being of a child, the responsibilities of parenthood are vast and complex. Understanding these responsibilities is essential for any individual considering becoming a parent, as well as for those who are already parents and looking to enhance their skills and knowledge in this area.

One of the most fundamental responsibilities of parenthood is to provide a safe and nurturing environment for a child to grow and develop. This includes ensuring that the child's basic needs, such as food, shelter, and clothing, are met, as well as creating a loving and supportive home environment. Parents should also strive to create an environment that is free from harm and danger, both physically and emotionally, by setting boundaries and monitoring the child's activities and interactions with others.

Another key responsibility of parenthood is to facilitate the child's emotional and social development. This involves providing love and support, as well as teaching the child how to navigate and express their emotions in a healthy and constructive manner. Parents also play a crucial role in shaping the child's social skills and helping them develop positive relationships with others. This can be achieved through modeling appropriate behavior, providing guidance and support, and encouraging the child to engage in social activities and interactions with peers.

In addition to emotional and social development, parents also have a responsibility to ensure the child's educational well-being. This includes supporting the child's learning and academic success, as well as advocating for their educational needs and interests. Parents should be actively involved in their child's education, communicating with teachers and school staff, monitoring progress, and providing additional support and resources as needed. By nurturing a love for learning and encouraging curiosity and exploration, parents can help their child succeed academically and develop a lifelong passion for education.

Beyond the physical, emotional, and educational needs of the child, parents also have a responsibility to instill values, morals, and ethics in their children. This involves teaching the child right from wrong, guiding them in making ethical decisions, and helping them develop a strong sense of integrity and empathy. Parents should also foster a sense of responsibility and accountability in their children, teaching them the importance of honesty, respect, and compassion towards others. By instilling these values and ethical principles, parents can help their children become caring, responsible, and ethical individuals who contribute positively to society.

In addition to the responsibilities outlined above, parents also play a crucial role in fostering independence and self-reliance in their children. This involves allowing the child to make decisions and mistakes, encouraging them to take risks and learn from their experiences, and providing opportunities for them to develop skills and competencies that will help them thrive in adulthood. By fostering independence and self-reliance, parents can help their children become confident, resilient, and capable individuals who are well-equipped to face the challenges of the world. By recognizing and embracing these responsibilities, parents can create a safe, nurturing, and supportive environment for their children to grow and thrive. Through love, support, guidance, and education, parents can help their children develop into confident, responsible, and ethical individuals who contribute positively to society. Parenthood is a rewarding and challenging journey, but by understanding and fulfilling these responsibilities, parents can ensure that their children reach their full potential and lead fulfilling lives.

- Importance of Developing Parenting Skills

Parenting is one of the most important and challenging roles that a person can undertake. It involves guiding, nurturing, and shaping the development of a child from infancy through adolescence and into young adulthood. Effective parenting requires a wide range of skills, including communication, discipline, empathy, problem-solving, and resilience. Developing these skills is crucial for ensuring that children grow up to be healthy, happy, and well-adjusted adults.

One of the key reasons why developing parenting skills is important is that it can have a significant impact on children's well-being and future success. Research has shown that children who grow up in homes where their parents have strong parenting skills are more likely to have better cognitive, social, and emotional development. They are also less likely to experience behavioral problems, mental health issues, or engage in risky behaviors. By honing their parenting skills, parents can create a safe and supportive environment where their children can thrive and reach their full potential.

In addition to benefiting children, developing parenting skills is also important for parents themselves. Parenting can be a stressful and demanding job, and having the necessary skills can help parents navigate the challenges that come with raising children. By learning how to communicate effectively, set boundaries, and manage conflict, parents can reduce their stress levels, improve their relationships with their children, and promote a positive family dynamic. Developing parenting skills can also increase parents' confidence and sense of competence, which can lead to a greater sense of fulfillment and satisfaction in their role as parents.

Furthermore, developing parenting skills is important for society as a whole. Children who grow up in stable and nurturing environments are more likely to become productive and responsible members of society. They are less likely to engage in criminal behavior, abuse drugs or alcohol, or experience poverty. By investing in parenting education and support programs, communities can help prevent social problems and promote the well-being of future generations. When parents have the tools and resources they need to be effective parents, everyone benefits.

There are many ways that parents can develop their parenting skills. One option is to participate in parenting classes or workshops, where they can learn from experts and gain valuable insights into effective parenting techniques. These classes often cover topics such as child development, discipline strategies, communication skills, and positive parenting techniques. Parents can also seek out books, articles, and online resources that provide information and guidance on parenting issues. By educating themselves about child development and parenting strategies, parents can enhance their skills and become more effective in their role.

Another important way for parents to develop their parenting skills is to seek support from other parents and professionals. Joining a parenting support group or seeking out counseling can provide parents with a safe space to share their experiences, learn from others, and receive guidance and encouragement. Working with a counselor or therapist can also help parents address any underlying issues or challenges that may be impacting their parenting abilities. By seeking help and support when needed, parents can improve their parenting skills and create a more positive and nurturing home environment for their children. By honing their communication, discipline, empathy, problem-solving, and resilience skills, parents can create a nurturing and supportive environment where their children can thrive and reach their full potential. Investing in parenting education and support programs can help parents acquire the knowledge and tools they need to be effective parents. By working together to promote positive parenting practices, we can create a brighter future for our children and our communities.

- The Impact of Parenting on Children's Development

Parenting plays a crucial role in shaping a child's development and overall well-being. Research has consistently shown that the quality of parenting children receive can have a profound impact on their emotional, social, and cognitive development. The relationship between parents and children is a critical factor that shapes children's self-esteem, emotional regulation, and social skills. Positive parenting practices, such as warmth, responsiveness, and consistency, have been associated with better outcomes for children across various domains of development.

One of the key aspects of parenting that influences children's development is the quality of attachment between parents and children. Attachment theory, developed by John Bowlby, posits that the quality of the early attachment relationship between a child and their primary caregiver lays the foundation for the child's social and emotional development. Secure attachment is characterized by the child feeling safe and supported in their relationship with their caregiver, while insecure attachment can lead to difficulties in emotional regulation and forming healthy relationships later in life. Parents who are sensitive, responsive, and attuned to their child's needs are more likely to foster secure attachment relationships, which have been associated with better emotional and social outcomes for children.

In addition to attachment, the parenting style adopted by parents also plays a significant role in shaping children's development. Researchers have identified four main parenting styles: authoritative, authoritarian, permissive, and neglectful. Authoritative parenting, which is characterized by high levels of warmth and responsiveness combined with clear and consistent rules and boundaries, has been consistently associated with positive outcomes for children. Children of authoritative parents tend to be more independent, self-regulated, and socially competent compared to children of authoritarian, permissive, or neglectful parents.

Moreover, the role of parental involvement in children's development cannot be understated. Parental involvement refers to the degree to which parents are actively engaged in their child's education, social activities, and overall well-being. Research has shown that children whose parents are involved in their lives and show a genuine interest in their activities tend to perform better academically, have higher levels of self-esteem, and engage in fewer risky behaviors. Parental involvement can take many forms, such as attending school events, helping with homework, and engaging in meaningful conversations with children about their interests and aspirations.

Furthermore, the impact of parenting on children's development extends beyond the early years and into adolescence and young adulthood. Parents continue to play a crucial role in shaping their children's development by providing guidance, support, and setting appropriate boundaries as their children navigate the challenges of growing up. Positive parenting practices, such as open communication, setting realistic expectations, and fostering independence, can help adolescents develop the skills and resilience needed to successfully transition into adulthood. Conversely, parents who are overly controlling or neglectful may hinder their children's ability to develop independence and autonomy. The quality of the parent-child relationship, the attachment style formed in early childhood, the parenting style adopted by parents, parental involvement, and the ongoing support and guidance provided by parents all contribute to shaping children's emotional, social, and cognitive development. By understanding the importance of parenting in child development and adopting positive parenting practices, parents can help their children thrive and reach their full potential. It is essential for parents to be aware of the impact their parenting style and practices have on their children and to actively strive to create a nurturing and supportive environment that fosters healthy development and well-being.

Chapter 2: Communication in Parenting

- Effective Communication Techniques

Effective communication is a critical skill in both personal and professional relationships. By mastering effective communication techniques, individuals can express themselves clearly, listen attentively, and build strong connections with others. In this discussion, we will explore some key strategies for improving communication skills and enhancing overall understanding and collaboration.

One of the most important aspects of effective communication is active listening. Active listening involves fully engaging with the speaker, paying attention to their words, tone, and body language, and showing empathy and understanding. By actively listening, individuals can demonstrate respect for the speaker and create a conducive environment for open and honest communication. This technique can help improve relationships, resolve conflicts, and foster trust and cooperation among team members.

Another essential communication technique is clarity and conciseness. It is important to express oneself clearly and concisely, avoiding jargon, ambiguity, or unnecessary details that may confuse the listener. By using simple language, organizing thoughts logically, and focusing on the key message, individuals can ensure that their communication is easily understood and effectively communicated. This technique is particularly important in professional settings, where clear and concise communication is essential for successful collaboration and decision-making.

Nonverbal communication is also a crucial aspect of effective communication. Nonverbal cues, such as facial expressions, gestures, and body language, can convey emotions, intentions, and attitudes that complement verbal communication. By being aware of and using nonverbal cues effectively, individuals can enhance their communication skills and improve their ability to connect with others. For example, maintaining eye contact, smiling, and using open body language can signal interest, engagement, and empathy, leading to improved understanding and rapport.

In addition to active listening, clarity and conciseness, and nonverbal communication, effective communication also involves emotional intelligence. Emotional intelligence refers to the ability to recognize, understand, and manage one's own emotions and the emotions of others. By developing emotional intelligence, individuals can communicate more effectively, build stronger relationships, and navigate conflicts and challenges with empathy and understanding. This skill is particularly important in professional settings, where emotional intelligence can contribute to effective leadership, teamwork, and problem-solving.

Furthermore, feedback and validation are essential components of effective communication. Providing feedback allows individuals to offer constructive criticism, praise, or guidance to others, helping them improve their performance, skills, or behavior. By giving feedback in a timely, specific, and constructive manner, individuals can create a supportive and growth-oriented environment that encourages learning and development. Validation, on the other hand, involves acknowledging and affirming the feelings, experiences, or perspectives of others. By validating others' emotions and experiences, individuals can build trust, empathy, and connection, leading to more meaningful and authentic communication.

Lastly, adaptability and flexibility are key attributes of effective communication. In an increasingly diverse and dynamic world, individuals must be able to adapt their communication style, approach, and methods to meet the needs and preferences of others. By being flexible and open-minded, individuals can adjust their communication techniques to accommodate different personality types, cultural backgrounds, and communication styles. This adaptability can help foster understanding, respect, and collaboration among individuals from various backgrounds and perspectives, leading to more inclusive and effective communication. By mastering active listening, clarity and conciseness, nonverbal communication, emotional intelligence, feedback and validation, and adaptability and flexibility, individuals can improve their communication skills and create more meaningful and authentic connections with others. These techniques are essential for navigating conflicts, resolving challenges, and achieving success in today's complex and interconnected world. By prioritizing effective communication, individuals can strengthen their relationships, enhance their teamwork, and cultivate a culture of open and honest communication in all aspects of their lives.

- Listening to Your Child

Listening is a vital component of effective communication, and this holds true when it comes to listening to your child. As parents, it is important to create a safe and open space for your child to express themselves without fear of judgment or criticism. By actively listening to your child, you are not only showing them that their thoughts and feelings are valid, but you are also building a strong foundation for a healthy parent-child relationship.

When it comes to listening to your child, it is important to approach the conversation with an open mind and without preconceived notions. Avoid interrupting or jumping to s, as this can hinder the flow of communication and prevent your child from fully expressing themselves. Instead, give your child your undivided attention and allow them to speak freely without any interruptions.

One key aspect of effective listening is empathy. Put yourself in your child's shoes and try to understand their perspective. By showing empathy, you are validating your child's emotions and showing them that you care about their feelings. This can go a long way in building trust and strengthening your relationship with your child.

Another important aspect of listening to your child is nonverbal communication. Pay attention to your child's body language, facial expressions, and tone of voice. These can provide valuable insights into how your child is feeling and what they are trying to communicate. By being attuned to these nonverbal cues, you can better understand your child and respond in a more empathetic and supportive manner.

It is also important to validate your child's feelings and experiences. Even if you may not agree with their perspective or emotions, it is crucial to acknowledge and validate their feelings. This does not mean that you have to agree with everything your child says, but rather that you are acknowledging and respecting their point of view.

In addition to listening actively and empathetically, it is important to create a safe and supportive environment for your child to express themselves. Encourage open communication and let your child know that they can come to you with any concerns or issues. By creating a safe space for your child to share their thoughts and feelings, you are fostering trust and building a strong bond with your child.

Listening to your child is not just about hearing what they have to say, but also about truly understanding and validating their emotions and experiences. By actively listening, showing empathy, and creating a supportive environment, you are strengthening your relationship with your child and fostering a sense of trust and open communication. Remember, listening is a two-way street, and by giving your child the space and support to express themselves, you are building a strong foundation for a healthy and positive parent-child relationship.

- Setting Healthy Boundaries

Setting healthy boundaries is an essential component of maintaining emotional and physical well-being in all aspects of life. Boundaries are the limits we set in relationships, both personal and professional, to protect ourselves and ensure that our needs are met. They define what is acceptable and unacceptable behavior from others and help us establish a sense of self-respect and self-worth. Without healthy boundaries, we may find ourselves feeling overwhelmed, resentful, and drained, as our needs are consistently being overlooked or disregarded. In order to cultivate healthy relationships and lead a fulfilling life, it is crucial to understand the importance of setting boundaries and to strive to establish and maintain them effectively.

One of the most significant benefits of setting healthy boundaries is the preservation of our mental and emotional well-being. By clearly defining what is acceptable and unacceptable behavior from others, we are able to protect ourselves from harm, both intentional and unintentional. Healthy boundaries help us to create a sense of safety and security in our relationships, as we establish limits that ensure our needs are respected and met. This can prevent us from feeling exploited, manipulated, or taken advantage of, as we are able to assert our own needs and desires with confidence and assertiveness.

Furthermore, setting healthy boundaries can also lead to improved communication and greater intimacy in relationships. When we are able to clearly express our needs and desires to others, we create an atmosphere of honesty and openness that fosters understanding and connection. By communicating our boundaries effectively, we can avoid misunderstandings, conflicts, and resentment, as we make our expectations and limits known to those around us. This can lead to deeper, more meaningful relationships, as both parties feel understood, respected, and valued in the relationship.

In addition to protecting our mental and emotional well-being, setting healthy boundaries also plays a crucial role in maintaining our physical health. When we establish clear limits and boundaries in our personal and professional lives, we are able to conserve our energy and avoid burnout. By saying no to activities, tasks, or relationships that drain us or cause us stress, we are able to prioritize self-care and focus on activities that nourish and energize us. This can prevent us from feeling overwhelmed, exhausted, or depleted, as we create space for rest, relaxation, and rejuvenation in our lives.

Moreover, setting healthy boundaries can also empower us to take control of our own lives and make decisions that align with our values and priorities. By clearly defining our limits and asserting our needs and desires, we are able to advocate for ourselves and advocate for what is important to us. This can help us to build self-confidence, assertiveness, and self-respect, as we take ownership of our lives and make choices that reflect our authentic selves. Setting and maintaining healthy boundaries can enable us to live more authentically and intentionally, as we create a life that is true to our values and aspirations. By establishing clear limits and asserting our needs and desires with confidence and assertiveness, we can protect ourselves from harm, improve communication and intimacy in relationships, conserve our energy and avoid burnout, and empower ourselves to make decisions that align with our values and priorities. As we strive to set and maintain healthy boundaries in all aspects of our lives, we can cultivate a greater sense of self-respect, self-worth, and authenticity, and create a life that is fulfilling, meaningful, and aligned with our true selves.

Chapter 3: Building a Strong Parent-Child Relationship

- Creating Bonds with Your Child

Creating strong bonds with your child is essential for their overall development and well-being. Research has shown that children who have secure attachments with their parents are more likely to have better social, emotional, and cognitive outcomes. Building a strong bond with your child can help foster a sense of trust, security, and love that will last a lifetime. There are several strategies and techniques that parents can use to create and strengthen bonds with their child, including positive communication, spending quality time together, and providing emotional support.

Positive communication is key to building a strong bond with your child. This involves actively listening to your child, showing empathy, and validating their feelings. By creating an open and supportive environment for communication, you can help your child feel comfortable sharing their thoughts and emotions with you. This can strengthen your relationship and help you better understand your child's needs and concerns. It is important to communicate with your child in a positive and respectful manner, using language that is age-appropriate and supportive. By listening to your child and responding with kindness and understanding, you can build trust and create a strong bond that will endure over time.

Spending quality time with your child is another important way to build a strong bond. Quality time does not have to be extravagant or expensive - it can be as simple as reading a book together, going for a walk, or playing a game. The key is to dedicate time to focus solely on your child and engage in activities that foster connection and closeness. By creating special moments together, you can strengthen your relationship and create lasting memories that your child will cherish. Quality time also provides opportunities for bonding, learning, and growth, and can help deepen your connection with your child.

Providing emotional support is essential for building a strong bond with your child. Children need to feel loved, nurtured, and supported by their parents in order to develop secure attachments. By being emotionally available and responsive to your child's needs, you can create a safe and nurturing environment that fosters trust and connection. It is important to validate your child's feelings, offer comfort and reassurance, and provide guidance and support when needed. By being there for your child emotionally, you can help them feel secure, valued, and loved, which can strengthen your bond and enhance their overall well-being.

In addition to positive communication, quality time, and emotional support, there are several other strategies that parents can use to create and strengthen bonds with their child. Building a strong bond with your child requires patience, consistency, and dedication. It is important to be present and attentive, to show interest and involvement in your child's life, and to be a positive role model. By providing love, support, and guidance, you can help your child develop a strong sense of security and self-esteem, and build a foundation for healthy relationships throughout their life. By using strategies such as positive communication, quality time, and emotional support, parents can build a strong and nurturing relationship with their child that will endure over time. Building a strong bond with your child is a process that requires time, effort, and dedication, but the rewards are immeasurable. By investing in your relationship with your child and prioritizing their emotional needs, you can create a deep and meaningful connection that will last a lifetime.

- Nurturing Trust and Respect

Developing trust and respect in any relationship, whether it be personal or professional, is essential for creating a positive and productive environment. Trust and respect go hand in hand, as one cannot exist without the other. Trust is built on a foundation of honesty, reliability, and integrity, while respect is earned through open communication, empathy, and understanding. When trust and respect are fostered, relationships flourish, leading to increased collaboration, loyalty, and overall satisfaction.

To nurture trust and respect in any relationship, it is crucial to prioritize open and honest communication. Transparency is key in building trust, as it allows individuals to feel secure in knowing that they are being kept informed and involved in decision-making processes. By communicating clearly and effectively, misunderstandings can be prevented, and everyone's needs and expectations can be understood and met. Without open communication, trust can easily be eroded, leading to a breakdown in the relationship.

In addition to communication, it is important to demonstrate reliability and consistency in order to build trust. When promises are kept and deadlines are met, individuals feel confident in relying on one another, knowing that they can count on each other to deliver. Consistency in behavior and actions also helps to build trust, as it shows that one's intentions are genuine and reliable. Trust is not built overnight, but rather through consistent effort and actions over time.

Respect is another crucial aspect of nurturing positive relationships. Respect is earned through listening, empathizing, and valuing the perspectives and opinions of others. By showing respect to others, individuals feel valued and appreciated, leading to a sense of mutual understanding and acceptance. Respect also involves setting healthy boundaries and treating others with dignity and empathy. When respect is mutual, relationships thrive and individuals feel comfortable expressing themselves and contributing their unique perspectives.

Empathy plays a key role in fostering trust and respect in relationships. By putting oneself in the shoes of others and understanding their feelings and perspectives, empathy builds a sense of connection and mutual understanding. Empathy also leads to increased communication and collaboration, as individuals feel heard and understood. When empathy is present, trust and respect naturally follow, as individuals feel valued and respected for who they are and what they bring to the table.

Building trust and respect in any relationship takes time and effort, but the rewards are well worth it. When trust and respect are present, relationships are stronger, more resilient, and more fulfilling. By prioritizing open communication, reliability, respect, and empathy, individuals can create a positive and productive environment where trust and respect thrive. With trust and respect as the foundation, relationships can withstand challenges and conflicts, leading to increased collaboration, creativity, and overall success. By nurturing trust and respect in our relationships, we build a strong and supportive community where everyone can thrive and grow.

- Fostering Love and Support

Fostering love and support is a fundamental aspect of building strong, healthy relationships in both personal and professional settings. In this context, fostering refers to the intentional cultivation and nurturing of feelings of care, empathy, and compassion towards others. Love, in this sense, goes beyond romantic feelings and encompasses a deep sense of connection, respect, and concern for the well-being of another individual. Support, on the other hand, involves providing practical assistance, emotional encouragement, and understanding to help someone navigate challenges and achieve their goals.

One of the key components of fostering love and support is effective communication. Clear and open communication is essential for building trust, establishing boundaries, and resolving conflicts in a respectful manner. Active listening, empathy, and validation are important skills that can help create a supportive environment where individuals feel heard and understood. By communicating openly and honestly, we can build stronger, more meaningful relationships based on mutual respect and understanding.

Another important aspect of fostering love and support is practicing empathy and compassion towards others. Empathy involves putting oneself in another person's shoes and trying to understand their perspective, feelings, and needs. By showing empathy, we can validate someone's experiences, offer comfort and support, and strengthen our emotional connection with them. Compassion, on the other hand, involves feeling concern for another person's well-being and taking action to help alleviate their suffering or distress. By practicing empathy and compassion in our relationships, we can create a more caring and supportive environment where individuals feel valued and respected.

In addition to communication and empathy, fostering love and support also involves creating a safe and inclusive space where individuals feel comfortable expressing themselves and seeking help when needed. Creating a sense of psychological safety, where individuals feel accepted, valued, and respected for who they are, is essential for fostering trust and building strong relationships. By creating a supportive environment where individuals feel free to be themselves, express their thoughts, feelings, and needs without fear of judgment or rejection, we can promote a culture of openness, honesty, and vulnerability that strengthens emotional connections and fosters love and support.

Furthermore, fostering love and support also involves setting and respecting boundaries in our relationships. Boundaries are essential for maintaining a healthy balance between giving and receiving support, protecting our own well-being, and respecting the autonomy and agency of others. By setting clear and healthy boundaries, we can establish mutual expectations, promote self-care, and prevent misunderstandings or conflicts in our relationships. Respecting boundaries is equally important, as it shows that we value and respect the autonomy and needs of others, and helps build trust and create a safe and supportive space where individuals feel empowered to communicate their boundaries and advocate for their needs. By practicing effective communication, empathy, compassion, creating a safe and inclusive environment, and setting and respecting boundaries, we can create a supportive and nurturing space where individuals feel valued, heard, and understood. In doing so, we can cultivate deeper emotional connections, promote well-being, and create a culture of love and support that enhances our personal and professional lives. By prioritizing love and support in our relationships, we can create a more caring and compassionate world where individuals can thrive and flourish.

Chapter 4: Discipline and Guidance

- Setting Clear Expectations

Setting clear expectations is a fundamental aspect of effective communication and successful collaboration in any relationship or organization. Whether it be in a professional setting, academic environment, or personal relationship, establishing clear expectations helps ensure that all parties involved are on the same page and working towards a common goal. By clearly defining roles, responsibilities, goals, and timelines, individuals can better understand what is expected of them and how their contributions fit into the larger picture. This not only fosters accountability and productivity but also helps prevent misunderstandings and conflicts that can arise when expectations are vague or unspoken.

In a professional setting, setting clear expectations is crucial for creating a productive and harmonious work environment. When employees are uncertain about their roles and responsibilities or have conflicting expectations from their supervisors or colleagues, it can lead to inefficiency, confusion, and ultimately, decreased morale. This clarity can also empower employees to take ownership of their work and make informed decisions that align with the company's objectives.

In an academic environment, setting clear expectations is equally important for promoting student success and engagement. When instructors clearly outline course objectives, expectations for assignments, grading criteria, and class policies, students are better equipped to plan their studies, manage their time effectively, and meet academic standards. Additionally, clear expectations can help students understand the learning outcomes of a course and how their efforts contribute to their academic growth and development. This can foster a sense of purpose and motivation, leading to increased student engagement and performance.

In personal relationships, setting clear expectations can help individuals navigate conflicts, manage boundaries, and build trust with one another. Whether in romantic relationships, friendships, or family dynamics, communicating openly and honestly about one's needs, boundaries, and preferences is essential for building healthy and supportive connections. By setting clear expectations around communication, emotional support, shared responsibilities, and personal boundaries, individuals can establish a mutual understanding of each other's needs and expectations. This can help prevent misunderstandings, resentments, and conflicts, ultimately fostering stronger and more fulfilling relationships. By taking the time to clarify roles, responsibilities, goals, and boundaries, individuals can establish a shared understanding of what is expected of them and how they can work together towards a common goal. This not only promotes accountability, efficiency, and mutual respect but also helps build trust, reduce misunderstandings, and create a positive and supportive environment for all parties involved. Whether in a professional, academic, or personal setting, setting clear expectations is a key ingredient for fostering healthy and successful relationships.

- Consistent Discipline Methods

Consistent discipline methods are a vital aspect of maintaining order and promoting positive behavior in any setting, whether it be in a classroom, workplace, or household. Consistency in discipline ensures that expectations are clearly communicated and enforced, creating a sense of fairness and stability for all individuals involved. By establishing clear rules and consequences, everyone knows what is expected of them and understands the potential outcomes of their actions.

One key aspect of consistent discipline methods is the establishment of clear and fair rules. Rules should be specific, reasonable, and easy to understand. They should also be consistent across all individuals and situations, so that everyone is held to the same standards. When rules are vague or arbitrarily enforced, it can lead to confusion, resentment, and a lack of respect for authority. By clearly outlining expectations and consequences, individuals are more likely to comply and understand the reasons behind the rules.

Consistency in discipline also requires a commitment to enforcing consequences when rules are broken. When consequences are consistently applied, individuals learn that their actions have real and predictable outcomes. This can help to shape behavior over time, as individuals come to understand the connection between their actions and the consequences that follow. Inconsistency in discipline can send mixed messages and undermine the efficacy of the rules, leading to confusion and frustration among those being disciplined.

Another important aspect of consistent discipline methods is the use of positive reinforcement in addition to consequences. While consequences are an important tool for shaping behavior, positive reinforcement can also be highly effective in promoting desired behaviors. By recognizing and rewarding positive behaviors, individuals are more likely to repeat them in the future. This can help to create a more positive and productive environment, where individuals are motivated to behave in ways that are in line with the established rules.

It is also important to consider the context and individual needs of those being disciplined when implementing consistent discipline methods. Different individuals may respond differently to various approaches, so it is important to tailor discipline methods to the specific situation and individual. This may require flexibility and a willingness to adapt strategies as needed. Additionally, it is important to consider the underlying reasons for behavior and address any underlying issues that may be contributing to negative behavior. By establishing clear rules, enforcing consequences, using positive reinforcement, and considering individual needs, discipline can be a powerful tool for shaping behavior and promoting a sense of fairness and order. Consistency in discipline helps to create a sense of stability and predictability, which is essential for maintaining a healthy and respectful environment. By being proactive and intentional in implementing consistent discipline methods, individuals can achieve greater success in shaping behavior and promoting positive outcomes.

- Teaching Positive Behavior

Teaching positive behavior is an important aspect of the educational process that helps students develop important social and emotional skills. Positive behavior refers to actions that are considered appropriate and beneficial in a social context. These behaviors include showing respect for others, cooperating with peers, following instructions, and demonstrating self-control. By teaching students positive behavior, educators can create a positive and productive learning environment that fosters academic success and personal development.

There are several strategies that educators can use to effectively teach positive behavior to students. One of the most important strategies is modeling positive behavior. Teachers should strive to be positive role models for their students by demonstrating the behaviors they want to see in their students. This can include being respectful to others, listening actively, and showing empathy towards others. By consistently modeling positive behavior, teachers can set a strong example for their students to follow.

In addition to modeling positive behavior, educators can also explicitly teach students the skills they need to exhibit positive behavior. This can involve teaching students social skills such as communication, conflict resolution, and problem-solving. By providing students with the tools they need to navigate social situations effectively, educators can empower students to make positive choices and build positive relationships with their peers.

Another important aspect of teaching positive behavior is providing students with consistent feedback and reinforcement. When students exhibit positive behavior, it is important for educators to recognize and praise them for their actions. Positive reinforcement can be a powerful motivator for students and can help to encourage them to continue exhibiting positive behavior. Conversely, when students engage in negative behavior, it is important for educators to address the behavior calmly and provide guidance on how to make better choices in the future.

It is also important for educators to create a positive and supportive classroom environment that encourages positive behavior. This can involve implementing clear expectations for behavior, establishing consistent routines, and providing students with opportunities to practice and develop their social skills. By creating a safe and supportive learning environment, educators can help students feel comfortable taking risks and making mistakes, which is essential for learning and growth.

In addition to teaching positive behavior in the classroom, educators can also involve parents and caregivers in the process. By working collaboratively with families, educators can help to reinforce positive behavior at home and provide consistent messaging to students about the importance of exhibiting positive behavior. This can involve sharing strategies for promoting positive behavior at home, providing resources for parents, and engaging in regular communication with families about their child's progress. By modeling positive behavior, explicitly teaching social skills, providing consistent feedback and reinforcement, creating a positive classroom environment, and involving parents and caregivers, educators can help students develop the necessary skills to navigate social situations effectively and build positive relationships with their peers. By prioritizing the teaching of positive behavior, educators can create a positive and inclusive learning environment where all students can thrive.

Chapter 5: Nurturing Emotional Intelligence

- Helping Your Child Manage Emotions

Emotional management is a crucial skill that children must learn in order to navigate the complexities of life. It is essential for their overall well-being and development. As parents, it is our responsibility to help our children understand and regulate their emotions effectively. By teaching them valuable coping mechanisms and strategies, we can empower them to handle challenging situations with grace and resilience.

One of the most important aspects of helping your child manage emotions is to create a safe and supportive environment where they feel comfortable expressing their feelings. Encourage open communication and actively listen to what your child has to say. Validate their emotions and let them know that it is okay to feel angry, sad, or frustrated. By acknowledging their feelings, you are helping them develop a sense of self-awareness and emotional intelligence.

It is also important to teach your child healthy ways to cope with their emotions. Encourage them to engage in activities that promote relaxation and stress relief, such as deep breathing exercises, mindfulness practices, or physical exercise. Help them identify triggers that lead to strong emotions and work together to develop strategies to manage them effectively. By teaching your child how to recognize and address their emotions in a constructive manner, you are laying the foundation for long-term emotional well-being.

Furthermore, it is important to model positive emotional management behaviors for your child. Children learn by example, so it is essential to practice what you preach. Show your child how to handle stress, anger, or sadness in a healthy way. Demonstrate the importance of patience, empathy, and resilience in the face of adversity. By showcasing these qualities, you are providing your child with a valuable template for navigating their own emotions.

In addition to providing emotional support and guidance, it is important to set clear boundaries and expectations for your child. Teach them the importance of self-regulation and impulse control. Help them understand that it is okay to feel strong emotions, but it is not okay to lash out or harm others as a result. By establishing boundaries and consequences for inappropriate behavior, you are teaching your child valuable lessons in emotional regulation and accountability.

In some cases, it may be necessary to seek professional help for your child if they are struggling to manage their emotions effectively. Therapy can be a useful tool for addressing underlying issues or learning new coping skills. A trained therapist can provide your child with the support and guidance they need to navigate their emotions in a healthy way. By creating a supportive environment, teaching healthy coping mechanisms, modeling positive behaviors, setting boundaries, and seeking professional help when needed, you can empower your child to develop the emotional intelligence and resilience they need to thrive in life. Remember that Rome wasn't built in a day, and emotional management is a skill that takes time and practice to master. Be patient with your child, and provide them with the love and support they need to navigate their emotions successfully.

- Teaching Empathy and Compassion

Empathy and compassion are two key qualities that play a crucial role in fostering positive relationships, promoting understanding, and creating a more harmonious society. As such, the importance of teaching empathy and compassion cannot be overstated. In this essay, we will delve into the concept of empathy and compassion, explore effective strategies for teaching these qualities, and discuss the benefits of cultivating empathy and compassion in both individuals and communities.

Empathy can be defined as the ability to understand and share the feelings of another person. It involves putting oneself in someone else's shoes and viewing the world from their perspective. Empathy allows individuals to connect with others on a deeper level, to build trust and rapport, and to foster meaningful relationships. Compassion, on the other hand, involves taking action to alleviate the suffering of others. It is characterized by a genuine concern for the well-being of others and a willingness to help those in need.

Teaching empathy and compassion is a multi-faceted process that involves both cognitive and emotional components. In order to effectively teach these qualities, it is important to first foster an understanding of what empathy and compassion are and why they are important. This can be done through discussions, readings, and activities that highlight the benefits of empathy and compassion in both personal and societal contexts. By helping individuals see the value of empathy and compassion, we can motivate them to cultivate these qualities in their own lives.

One effective strategy for teaching empathy and compassion is through the use of role-playing exercises. These exercises allow individuals to actively engage in situations where empathy and compassion are required, allowing them to practice these qualities in a safe and supportive environment. Role-playing exercises can help individuals develop their emotional intelligence, build their capacity for empathy, and strengthen their ability to connect with others on a deeper level.

Another important aspect of teaching empathy and compassion is helping individuals develop their capacity for self-reflection. By encouraging individuals to reflect on their own thoughts, feelings, and actions, we can help them develop a greater awareness of themselves and their impact on others. This self-awareness can be a powerful tool for building empathy and compassion, as individuals begin to see the connections between their own experiences and the experiences of others.

In addition to individual reflection, it is important to create opportunities for group discussions and collaborative activities that promote empathy and compassion. By engaging in dialogue with others and working together towards common goals, individuals can develop a greater sense of empathy and compassion for their peers. These interactions can also help individuals see the value of diversity and inclusion, and build bridges across differences to create a more cohesive and inclusive community.

One of the key benefits of cultivating empathy and compassion is the impact it can have on mental health and well-being. Research has shown that individuals who are more empathetic and compassionate tend to experience lower levels of stress, anxiety, and depression. By fostering empathy and compassion in individuals, we can help them build resilience, cope with challenges, and navigate the complexities of modern life with greater ease.

Moreover, teaching empathy and compassion can also lead to a more cohesive and harmonious society. By promoting understanding and empathy between individuals, we can foster greater social cohesion, reduce conflict, and build a more inclusive and tolerant community. Empathy and compassion can help bridge divides, promote dialogue and understanding, and create a more supportive and compassionate society for all. By highlighting the importance of empathy and compassion, engaging individuals in role-playing exercises, promoting self-reflection, and facilitating group discussions, we can help individuals develop these essential qualities and reap the many benefits they offer. Ultimately, by cultivating empathy and compassion in individuals and communities, we can build a more empathetic, compassionate, and inclusive society for all.

- Encouraging Emotional Expression

Encouraging emotional expression is a crucial aspect of fostering healthy communication and relationships. Emotions play a significant role in how we perceive and respond to the world around us, and being able to express our feelings effectively can lead to greater understanding and connection with others. However, many people struggle with expressing their emotions for a variety of reasons, including societal norms, fear of judgment, or lack of emotional intelligence. It is important to create an environment where individuals feel safe and supported in sharing their feelings openly and honestly.

One way to encourage emotional expression is by fostering a culture of emotional intelligence within a community or organization. Emotional intelligence is the ability to recognize, understand, and manage one's own emotions, as well as the emotions of others. By developing emotional intelligence skills, individuals can express their feelings in a constructive and empathetic manner, leading to improved communication and conflict resolution. This can be done through workshops, training programs, or even regular check-ins to discuss feelings and emotions within a group setting.

Another way to promote emotional expression is by creating space for open and honest communication. This means actively listening to others without judgement, providing validation and empathy, and offering support when needed. By creating a safe and non-judgmental environment, individuals are more likely to feel comfortable sharing their emotions and experiences. This can be done through active listening techniques, such as reflecting back what someone has said or asking clarifying questions to show that you are engaged and interested in their feelings.

In addition to fostering emotional intelligence and creating a safe space for communication, it is important to validate and normalize all emotions, including those that may be perceived as negative or uncomfortable. Emotions are a normal and natural part of the human experience, and it is important to acknowledge and accept them without judgment. By validating one's emotions, you are acknowledging their feelings and showing that you understand and empathize with their experiences. This can help individuals feel heard and supported, leading to greater trust and emotional connection within relationships.

Encouraging emotional expression also involves helping individuals develop healthy coping mechanisms for managing their emotions. This may include practicing mindfulness techniques, engaging in physical activities, journaling, or seeking professional help when needed. By teaching individuals how to effectively manage their emotions, they can learn to express themselves in a healthy and constructive manner. By developing emotional intelligence, creating a safe space for communication, validating all emotions, and promoting healthy coping mechanisms, individuals can learn to express themselves in a meaningful and constructive way. This can lead to greater understanding, empathy, and connection with others, ultimately leading to more fulfilling and harmonious relationships.

Chapter 6: Encouraging Independence

- Promoting Self-Reliance

Self-reliance is a key concept that is often emphasized in various fields such as psychology, education, and business. It refers to an individual's ability to rely on oneself for guidance, support, and decision-making, rather than depending on others. Promoting self-reliance is important for overall personal growth, development, and success in life.

One of the main benefits of promoting self-reliance is the empowerment and independence that individuals gain. When individuals are self-reliant, they feel more in control of their lives and are less likely to be swayed by external influences. This sense of empowerment can lead to increased self-confidence, self-esteem, and self-worth. With these qualities, individuals are better equipped to face challenges and overcome obstacles that come their way.

Another advantage of promoting self-reliance is the development of critical thinking and decision-making skills. When individuals are encouraged to rely on themselves, they are forced to think through situations, analyze options, and make informed decisions. This process of critical thinking and decision-making not only helps individuals solve problems effectively but also enhances their overall cognitive abilities.

Furthermore, promoting self-reliance fosters a sense of accountability and responsibility. When individuals are self-reliant, they take ownership of their actions and choices. They are less likely to blame external factors or other people for their failures or shortcomings. This sense of accountability and responsibility not only enhances individual integrity but also builds trust and credibility with others.

In addition, promoting self-reliance can lead to increased resilience and adaptability. When individuals are used to facing challenges on their own, they become better equipped to handle setbacks, failures, and adversity. They learn to bounce back from difficult situations and adapt to changing circumstances. This resilience and adaptability are essential qualities for success in both personal and professional life.

It is important to note that promoting self-reliance does not mean isolating oneself or refusing help from others. It is about finding the right balance between independence and interdependence. In fact, individuals who are self-reliant are often more willing to seek support and collaborate with others when needed. They are able to maintain healthy relationships while still maintaining their sense of autonomy and self-reliance. By empowering individuals to rely on themselves, we can foster independence, critical thinking, accountability, resilience, and adaptability. Ultimately, promoting self-reliance is a key component of building a strong foundation for individuals to thrive in all aspects of their lives.

- Allowing for Personal Growth

Personal growth is a fundamental aspect of human development that encompasses various dimensions of an individual's life, including emotional, intellectual, social, and spiritual growth. It involves the continuous process of self-improvement, self-discovery, and self-awareness, leading to a deeper understanding of oneself and the world around us. Allowing for personal growth means being open to new experiences, challenges, and opportunities that promote learning and development.

One key element of personal growth is self-reflection, which involves taking the time to examine one's thoughts, feelings, and behaviors in order to gain insight into oneself and identify areas for improvement. This process allows individuals to better understand their strengths, weaknesses, values, and beliefs, and to make meaningful changes in their lives. Self-reflection can be achieved through various practices, such as journaling, meditation, mindfulness, and therapy, all of which help individuals to develop a deeper sense of self-awareness and self-compassion.

Another important aspect of personal growth is setting and achieving personal goals. By establishing clear and achievable goals, individuals can create a roadmap for their personal development and track their progress over time. Goal-setting provides a sense of direction and purpose, motivates individuals to take action, and fosters a sense of accomplishment and satisfaction when goals are achieved. It is important for individuals to set goals that are specific, measurable, achievable, relevant, and time-bound in order to increase their chances of success and promote continuous self-improvement.

In addition to self-reflection and goal-setting, personal growth also involves stepping out of one's comfort zone and embracing new challenges and opportunities for learning and growth. By pushing oneself beyond familiar boundaries and trying new experiences, individuals can expand their horizons, develop new skills and knowledge, and gain a greater sense of self-confidence and resilience. Embracing challenges, whether they are small or large, can lead to personal growth and transformation, as individuals learn to adapt to new situations, overcome obstacles, and grow from their experiences.

It is important for individuals to cultivate a growth mindset in order to foster personal growth and development. A growth mindset is the belief that one's talents, abilities, and intelligence can be developed through effort, practice, and learning. Individuals with a growth mindset are more likely to embrace challenges, persist in the face of setbacks, seek feedback and criticism, and view mistakes as opportunities for learning and growth. By cultivating a growth mindset, individuals can overcome self-limiting beliefs and attitudes, cultivate a sense of resilience and optimism, and unlock their full potential for personal growth and success. Personal growth is a lifelong journey that requires individuals to be open to new experiences, opportunities, and learning, in order to continue evolving and improving as individuals. By fostering self-awareness, setting goals, stepping out of one's comfort zone, and cultivating a growth mindset, individuals can unlock their full potential, achieve their personal goals, and lead fulfilling and meaningful lives. Embracing personal growth is not only beneficial for individuals but also for society as a whole, as it leads to greater self-fulfillment, well-being, and positive impact on others.

- Balancing Guidance and Freedom

Achieving a balance between providing guidance and allowing freedom is essential in various aspects of life, including education, parenting, and leadership. This delicate equilibrium requires careful consideration of individual needs and expectations while fostering growth, independence, and personal development. It is crucial to understand that too much guidance can stifle creativity, autonomy, and decision-making skills, while excessive freedom may lead to confusion, lack of direction, and disorganization. Striking the right balance involves establishing clear boundaries, setting expectations, offering support and encouragement, and allowing individuals the flexibility to explore, learn, and make mistakes.

In the realm of education, striking a balance between providing guidance and allowing freedom is critical for fostering a conducive learning environment that promotes creativity, critical thinking, and self-directed learning. Teachers play a vital role in guiding students through the learning process, providing them with necessary instructions, resources, and support while allowing them the freedom to explore, experiment, and discover knowledge on their own. By striking the right balance between guidance and freedom, educators can empower students to take ownership of their learning, develop problem-solving skills, and cultivate a lifelong love for learning.

Similarly, in the context of parenting, achieving a balance between providing guidance and allowing freedom is essential for nurturing healthy relationships, fostering independence, and promoting emotional and social development in children. Parents need to strike a balance between setting boundaries, instilling values, and providing guidance, while also allowing children the freedom to express themselves, make decisions, and learn from their experiences. By striking the right balance between guidance and freedom, parents can foster trust, respect, and open communication with their children, while also promoting autonomy, self-confidence, and resilience.

In the realm of leadership, achieving a balance between providing guidance and allowing freedom is crucial for motivating, inspiring, and empowering individuals to achieve their full potential and contribute to the success of the organization. Effective leaders need to strike a balance between providing clear direction, setting goals, and offering support and guidance, while also allowing team members the freedom to innovate, take risks, and make decisions autonomously. By striking the right balance between guidance and freedom, leaders can create a positive and productive work environment that encourages creativity, collaboration, and continuous growth and development. By striking the right balance between guidance and freedom, individuals can empower themselves and others to explore, learn, and grow, while also fostering trust, respect, and collaboration. It is through this delicate equilibrium that we can create a positive and supportive environment that promotes creativity, autonomy, and self-discovery, ultimately leading to personal and professional success.

Chapter 7: Handling Challenges and Conflict

- Resolving Parent-Child Conflicts

Parent-child conflicts are a common occurrence in families, and they can arise from a variety of factors such as differing personalities, communication styles, or values. These conflicts can range from minor disagreements to more serious issues that can strain the relationship between parent and child. However, it is important to address these conflicts in a timely and effective manner in order to maintain a healthy and positive relationship with your child.

One of the key factors to resolving parent-child conflicts is effective communication. It is important for parents to listen to their child's perspective and feelings without interrupting or dismissing them. By actively listening and validating their feelings, parents can demonstrate empathy and create a safe space for their child to express themselves. It is also important for parents to communicate their own thoughts and feelings in a calm and respectful manner, avoiding blame or criticism. By fostering open and honest communication, parents and children can work towards understanding each other's perspectives and finding common ground.

In addition to effective communication, setting boundaries and expectations can also help to prevent and resolve conflicts between parents and children. By establishing clear rules and consequences, parents can provide structure and guidance for their child, and help to prevent misunderstandings or disagreements. It is important for parents to be consistent in enforcing these boundaries, and to communicate them clearly to their child. By setting boundaries and expectations, parents can create a sense of security and predictability for their child, and reduce the likelihood of conflicts arising.

Furthermore, it is essential for parents to show empathy and understanding towards their child during conflicts. Parents should try to see things from their child's perspective, and validate their feelings and experiences. By acknowledging their child's emotions and demonstrating empathy, parents can create a sense of connection and trust with their child. It is important for parents to remain calm and composed during conflicts, and to avoid reacting impulsively or emotionally. By showing empathy and understanding, parents can help to de-escalate conflicts and create a more positive and constructive atmosphere for resolving issues.

In addition to effective communication, setting boundaries, and showing empathy, it is important for parents to work towards finding solutions and compromises during conflicts with their child. Instead of trying to win the argument or impose their point of view, parents should focus on finding common ground and working together towards a resolution. This may involve brainstorming ideas, listening to each other's perspectives, and finding creative solutions that meet both parties' needs. By collaborating and problem-solving together, parents and children can work towards resolving conflicts in a constructive and positive way.

It is also important for parents to reflect on their own behavior and attitudes during conflicts with their child. Parents should be willing to acknowledge their own mistakes and take responsibility for their actions, and to model accountability and self-reflection for their child. By demonstrating humility and a willingness to learn and grow, parents can create a healthy and respectful environment for resolving conflicts with their child. It is important for parents to be open to feedback and to be willing to make changes in their behavior or communication style in order to improve their relationship with their child. By approaching conflicts with an open mind and a willingness to listen and learn, parents can create a healthy and positive relationship with their child. Conflict is a natural part of any relationship, and it is important for parents and children to work together towards resolving conflicts in a constructive and respectful manner. By fostering open and honest communication, setting clear boundaries and expectations, demonstrating empathy and understanding, finding solutions and compromises, and reflecting on one's own behavior, parents can navigate conflicts with their child in a way that promotes growth, understanding, and connection.

- Dealing with Behavior Issues

Dealing with behavior issues is a complex and multifaceted task that educators, parents, and caregivers often face when working with children and adolescents. Behavior issues can manifest in a variety of ways, such as defiance, aggression, withdrawal, or other challenging behaviors. It is important to approach these issues with empathy, understanding, and a proactive mindset in order to effectively address and manage them. This article will explore some strategies and techniques that can be used to help deal with behavior issues in a positive and constructive manner.

One of the first steps in dealing with behavior issues is to establish a positive and supportive relationship with the child or adolescent. Building trust and rapport is essential in creating a safe and nurturing environment where the individual feels comfortable expressing themselves and sharing their concerns. By showing empathy and understanding, caregivers and educators can help the child or adolescent feel heard and validated, which can in turn reduce the likelihood of further behavioral issues arising.

It is also important to establish clear and consistent boundaries and expectations when dealing with behavior issues. Setting clear rules and consequences can help provide structure and guidance for the child or adolescent, and can help them understand the expectations for their behavior. Consistency is key when enforcing rules and consequences, as it helps to reinforce the message and ensures that the individual knows what to expect if they engage in inappropriate behavior.

When addressing behavior issues, it is important to consider the underlying factors that may be contributing to the challenging behavior. Children and adolescents may act out for a variety of reasons, such as stress, trauma, anxiety, or other emotional and psychological factors. By taking the time to understand the root causes of the behavior, caregivers and educators can better address the underlying issues and provide appropriate support and intervention.

In some cases, behavior issues may be a sign of an underlying mental health condition or developmental disorder. It is important to seek professional help and guidance if there are concerns about a child or adolescent's behavior. A mental health professional can help provide a comprehensive assessment and identification of any underlying issues, and can provide recommendations for appropriate treatment and intervention.

When dealing with behavior issues, it is important to focus on positive reinforcement and praise for good behavior. By acknowledging and rewarding positive behaviors, caregivers and educators can help reinforce and encourage the desired behaviors in the child or adolescent. This can help build self-esteem and confidence, and can motivate the individual to continue exhibiting positive behavior.

It is also important to teach and model appropriate social and emotional skills when dealing with behavior issues. Children and adolescents may not always have the necessary skills to regulate their emotions, communicate effectively, or resolve conflicts in a positive manner. By teaching and modeling these skills, caregivers and educators can help the individual develop the necessary tools to navigate social interactions and manage their emotions in a healthy way. By establishing a positive and supportive relationship, setting clear boundaries and expectations, addressing underlying factors, seeking professional help when necessary, using positive reinforcement, and teaching and modeling appropriate social and emotional skills, caregivers and educators can help empower children and adolescents to make positive choices and develop healthy behaviors.

- Seeking Support and Resources

Seeking support and resources is an essential aspect of personal and professional growth. It is important to recognize when you need help or guidance in order to reach your full potential. Whether you are facing a challenging situation at work, school, or in your personal life, seeking the right support can make a significant difference in your ability to overcome obstacles and achieve success.

One of the first steps in seeking support and resources is to identify the specific areas in which you need assistance. This could involve seeking help with technical skills, emotional support, or guidance on career advancement. By pinpointing the areas that require attention, you can then begin to explore the various resources available to you.

There are numerous resources available to individuals seeking support in various aspects of their lives. These resources can include mentors, coaches, counselors, support groups, online forums, and professional organizations. Each of these resources can provide different types of assistance and guidance, depending on your specific needs.

Mentors can be invaluable sources of support and guidance, especially in a professional setting. A mentor can offer insights and advice based on their own experiences, helping you navigate challenges and make informed decisions. In addition to mentors, coaches can also provide valuable support in helping you develop specific skills or strategies to achieve your goals.

Counselors and therapists can offer emotional support and guidance for individuals facing personal challenges or mental health issues. Support groups can provide a sense of community and connection with others who are experiencing similar struggles. Online forums and professional organizations can offer resources and networking opportunities for those seeking to advance their careers or skills.

It is important to approach seeking support and resources with an open mind and willingness to learn. Recognizing that you may not have all the answers or solutions to your challenges is the first step in seeking help. By being open to new ideas and perspectives, you can benefit from the diverse range of resources available to you.

In addition to seeking support from external resources, it is also important to cultivate a sense of self-awareness and resilience. Building a strong foundation of self-awareness can help you better understand your strengths and areas for growth, allowing you to seek the right support and resources to help you improve.

Resilience is another key aspect of seeking support and resources. It is important to develop the ability to bounce back from setbacks and remain focused on your goals, even in the face of challenges. By fostering a sense of resilience, you can better navigate obstacles and setbacks on your journey to personal and professional growth. By identifying your specific needs and exploring the various resources available to you, you can gain the assistance and guidance needed to overcome challenges and achieve success. Approach seeking support with an open mind and willingness to learn, and cultivate self-awareness and resilience to navigate obstacles along the way. With the right support and resources, you can reach your full potential and thrive in all aspects of your life.

Chapter 8: Supporting Your Child's Education

- Fostering a Love for Learning

Fostering a love for learning is a vital aspect of education that all educators and parents should prioritize. When students develop a genuine passion for learning, they are more likely to excel academically, engage in critical thinking, and continue their quest for knowledge throughout their lives. In order to foster a love for learning, educators and parents must create a supportive and stimulating environment that encourages curiosity, exploration, and personal growth.

One of the key strategies for fostering a love for learning is to create a positive and nurturing learning environment. This includes establishing clear expectations, providing consistent support, and fostering a sense of belonging and connection among students. When students feel safe, respected, and valued in their learning environment, they are more likely to develop a positive attitude towards learning and be motivated to explore new ideas and concepts. It is important for educators and parents to create a welcoming and inclusive atmosphere where students feel comfortable taking risks, making mistakes, and asking questions.

Another important factor in fostering a love for learning is to make learning meaningful and relevant to students' lives. This can be achieved by connecting the curriculum to real-world issues, experiences, and interests of students. When students see the value and relevance of what they are learning, they are more likely to become engaged, motivated, and invested in their education. Educators and parents can also help students make connections between different subjects and disciplines, showing them how learning is interconnected and interdisciplinary.

In addition to creating a positive and meaningful learning environment, educators and parents can also foster a love for learning by encouraging and celebrating students' efforts and achievements. By providing positive feedback, praise, and recognition for students' hard work, creativity, and perseverance, educators and parents can help nurture students' self-confidence, self-esteem, and intrinsic motivation. It is important to recognize and celebrate students' diverse talents, strengths, and learning styles, and to provide opportunities for them to showcase their learning and achievements.

Furthermore, fostering a love for learning also involves promoting a growth mindset and resilience among students. Educators and parents can help students develop a growth mindset by teaching them that intelligence, abilities, and talents are not fixed, but can be developed through effort, practice, and learning from mistakes. By encouraging students to embrace challenges, persevere through setbacks, and embrace the learning process as a journey of self-discovery and growth, educators and parents can help empower students to take ownership of their learning and become lifelong learners. By creating a positive and nurturing learning environment, making learning meaningful and relevant, encouraging and celebrating students' efforts and achievements, promoting a growth mindset and resilience, educators and parents can help cultivate a love for learning that will empower students to excel academically, engage in critical thinking, and continue their quest for knowledge throughout their lives. Ultimately, fostering a love for learning is not only about acquiring knowledge and skills, but also about developing a lifelong passion for learning, personal growth, and self-discovery.

- Encouraging Academic Success

Academic success is a multifaceted concept that encompasses not only achieving high grades, but also developing a deep understanding of the material, honing critical thinking skills, and fostering a passion for lifelong learning. While academic success can look different for every individual, there are several key strategies that can help students excel in their academic pursuits.

One of the most important factors in encouraging academic success is creating a supportive and nurturing learning environment. This can take many forms, from providing access to resources such as tutoring services and study groups, to fostering a culture of collaboration and intellectual curiosity. By creating an atmosphere where students feel comfortable asking questions, making mistakes, and exploring new ideas, educators can help them develop the confidence and motivation needed to excel academically.

In addition to a supportive learning environment, it is also important to set clear and realistic academic goals. By setting specific, measurable, achievable, relevant, and time-bound (SMART) goals, students can create a roadmap for their academic success and track their progress along the way. This can help students stay focused and motivated, as well as provide them with a sense of accomplishment as they work towards achieving their goals.

Another key factor in encouraging academic success is developing strong study skills and time management techniques. These skills are essential for helping students stay organized, prioritize their workload, and effectively prepare for exams and assignments. By teaching students how to effectively manage their time, set priorities, and break tasks into manageable chunks, educators can help them develop the discipline and resilience needed to succeed academically.

Furthermore, it is important for students to cultivate a growth mindset and embrace the concept of continuous improvement. By viewing challenges as opportunities for growth and learning, rather than obstacles to be overcome, students can develop a positive attitude towards their academic work and build resilience in the face of setbacks. This mindset can help students develop a sense of agency and ownership over their learning, as well as foster a lifelong love of learning that extends far beyond the classroom. By providing students with the resources, tools, and mindset needed to excel academically, educators can help them reach their full potential and achieve success in their academic pursuits. By fostering a culture of collaboration, curiosity, and continuous improvement, educators can empower students to become lifelong learners who are equipped to succeed in their academic and professional endeavors.

- Communicating with Teachers and Schools

Effective communication between teachers and schools is a crucial component of a successful academic experience for students. It is essential for parents, teachers, and administrators to work together to provide the best possible support for children's learning and development. Clear and open lines of communication can help to ensure that students receive the resources and assistance they need to thrive in the classroom.

One of the key aspects of communicating with teachers and schools is establishing regular and proactive communication channels. Parents should make an effort to attend parent-teacher conferences, school events, and other opportunities to meet with teachers and school staff. These interactions provide a valuable opportunity to discuss their child's progress, address any concerns, and work together to create a plan for supporting the child's academic and social development. By building positive relationships with teachers and school administrators, parents can establish a strong foundation for collaboration and communication.

In addition to in-person communication, technology can also play a valuable role in facilitating communication between teachers, schools, and parents. Many schools now use online portals and apps to provide parents with access to important information about their child's academics, attendance, and behavior. These tools can be a convenient way for parents to stay informed about their child's progress and to communicate with teachers outside of regular school hours. By utilizing these technological resources, parents can stay more actively engaged in their child's education and provide valuable support to teachers and schools.

Another important aspect of effective communication with teachers and schools is being proactive about addressing any concerns or questions that arise. If a parent has a concern about their child's academic progress, behavior, or social interactions at school, it is important to address it promptly and directly with the teacher or school administrator. By openly communicating their concerns and working together to find a solution, parents can help to ensure that their child receives the support they need to succeed in the classroom. It is also important for parents to keep the lines of communication open and to follow up on any issues or concerns to ensure that they are effectively addressed.

In addition to addressing concerns, it is also important for parents to provide feedback to teachers and schools about their child's progress and the effectiveness of their educational programs. By sharing their insights and perspectives, parents can help teachers and administrators to better understand their child's needs and to make any necessary adjustments to their instruction or support. This feedback can be a valuable tool for improving the quality of education and support that students receive, and can help to strengthen the partnership between parents, teachers, and schools.

To conclude, it is important for parents, teachers, and schools to approach communication with a spirit of collaboration and partnership. By working together as a team, parents and educators can create a supportive and cohesive learning environment that maximizes the potential for student success. This collaborative approach can help to foster mutual respect and understanding, and can lead to more effective communication and problem-solving. By prioritizing clear and open communication, parents, teachers, and schools can create a positive and productive relationship that benefits the entire school community. By establishing regular and proactive communication channels, utilizing technology tools, addressing concerns promptly, providing feedback, and fostering a spirit of collaboration, parents can work together with teachers and schools to provide the best possible support for their child's education. By prioritizing communication and partnership, parents, teachers, and schools can create a strong and supportive learning environment that helps students to reach their full potential.

Chapter 9: Creating a Healthy Lifestyle

- Promoting Physical and Mental Well-Being

Promoting physical and mental well-being is essential for maintaining a healthy and fulfilling life. It involves taking care of both the body and mind, and finding a balance between physical activity, nutrition, relaxation, and mental health practices. By prioritizing well-being, individuals can reduce the risk of chronic diseases, improve their overall quality of life, and enhance their resilience to stress and challenges.

One of the key components of promoting physical well-being is engaging in regular exercise. Physical activity has numerous benefits for the body, including improved cardiovascular health, weight management, and enhanced muscle strength and flexibility. Exercise also releases endorphins, which are chemicals in the brain that act as natural mood lifters and reduce feelings of stress and anxiety. Incorporating regular exercise into your routine, whether it's through cardio, strength training, yoga, or other forms of physical activity, can help boost your energy levels, improve your mood, and increase your overall sense of well-being.

In addition to physical activity, maintaining a balanced and nutritious diet is crucial for promoting physical well-being. Eating a variety of fruits, vegetables, whole grains, lean proteins, and healthy fats can provide essential nutrients and fuel for the body to function optimally. It's important to pay attention to portion sizes, limit processed foods and added sugars, and stay hydrated by drinking plenty of water throughout the day. Making small, sustainable changes to your diet can have a big impact on your overall health and well-being.

Alongside physical well-being, mental well-being plays a significant role in promoting overall wellness. Mental health practices such as mindfulness meditation, journaling, therapy, and social support can help individuals manage stress, anxiety, and other mental health challenges. Taking time to prioritize self-care and engage in activities that bring joy and relaxation can also have a positive impact on mental well-being. By practicing self-compassion, setting boundaries, and seeking help when needed, individuals can strengthen their mental resilience and emotional well-being.

Another important aspect of promoting physical and mental well-being is getting an adequate amount of sleep. Sleep is essential for the body to repair and reset, as well as for cognitive functioning, mood regulation, and overall health. Establishing a consistent sleep routine, creating a relaxing bedtime routine, and creating a comfortable sleep environment can help improve sleep quality and promote overall well-being. If you're struggling with sleep issues, it's important to speak with a healthcare provider to address any underlying factors and find the right strategies to improve your sleep. By engaging in regular exercise, maintaining a balanced diet, practicing mental health strategies, and prioritizing self-care, individuals can enhance their overall quality of life, reduce the risk of chronic diseases, and build resilience to stress and challenges. By making small, sustainable changes to your daily routine and seeking support when needed, you can take proactive steps to promote your physical and mental well-being for a healthier and happier life.

- Encouraging Healthy Habits

Encouraging healthy habits is essential for maintaining overall well-being and preventing chronic diseases. Healthy habits encompass a wide range of behaviors, including eating a balanced diet, exercising regularly, getting enough sleep, managing stress, and avoiding harmful substances such as tobacco and excessive alcohol. These habits not only contribute to physical health but also play a significant role in mental and emotional well-being. By adopting and maintaining healthy habits, individuals can improve their quality of life and reduce their risk of developing health issues in the future.

One of the key strategies for encouraging healthy habits is education. Providing people with accurate information about the benefits of healthy habits and the risks associated with unhealthy behaviors can motivate them to make positive changes in their lives. This education can take many forms, such as public health campaigns, workplace wellness programs, and community health initiatives. By raising awareness about the importance of healthy habits and providing resources and support to help individuals make healthy choices, we can empower people to take control of their health and well-being.

In addition to education, social support can also play a crucial role in encouraging healthy habits. Research has shown that people are more likely to adopt and maintain healthy behaviors when they have the support of friends, family, and community members. This support can come in many forms, including encouragement, accountability, and practical assistance. By creating a supportive environment that promotes healthy habits, we can help individuals overcome barriers and obstacles that may prevent them from making positive changes in their lives.

Another effective strategy for encouraging healthy habits is setting realistic goals and tracking progress. By setting specific, achievable goals and monitoring their progress over time, individuals can stay motivated and focused on making healthy choices. This can help them build momentum and stay on track, even when faced with challenges or setbacks. Tracking progress can also provide valuable feedback on what is working and what may need to be adjusted, allowing individuals to make informed decisions about their health and well-being.

In addition to education, social support, and goal setting, creating a supportive environment that makes healthy choices easy and accessible can also encourage healthy habits. This can include things like providing access to healthy food options, encouraging physical activity through workplace or community programs, and promoting policies that support health and well-being. By making healthy choices the default option in our environments, we can help individuals make healthier decisions without having to rely solely on willpower or self-control.

Ultimately, encouraging healthy habits requires a multifaceted approach that addresses the complex factors that influence behavior. By combining education, social support, goal setting, and environmental changes, we can create a culture that values health and well-being and empowers individuals to make positive choices for themselves and their communities. With the right resources and support, individuals can build the habits they need to live healthy, fulfilling lives and prevent chronic diseases in the long run. By working together to promote healthy habits, we can create a healthier, happier society for generations to come.

- Modeling Self-Care

Self-care is a term that has gained increasing recognition in recent years as a crucial component of overall well-being and mental health. It encompasses a wide range of practices and activities that individuals engage in to promote their physical, emotional, and psychological well-being. Self-care is not simply about pampering oneself or indulging in luxuries; rather, it is about taking intentional steps to prioritize one's own needs and nurture oneself in a holistic manner. Modeling self-care involves setting an example for others by demonstrating healthy self-care practices and encouraging others to prioritize their own well-being.

One key aspect of modeling self-care is recognizing the importance of setting boundaries and taking time for oneself. In a society that often glorifies busyness and productivity, it can be easy to neglect one's own needs in favor of meeting external demands. However, without taking time to rest and recharge, individuals risk burning out and experiencing negative consequences for their mental and physical health. By modeling healthy boundaries and self-care practices, individuals can show others that it is not only acceptable but necessary to prioritize self-care.

Another important aspect of modeling self-care is practicing self-compassion and self-acceptance. Many people struggle with feelings of unworthiness or self-criticism, which can undermine their ability to take care of themselves. By demonstrating self-compassion and self-acceptance, individuals can show others that it is possible to treat oneself with kindness and understanding, even in the face of challenges or setbacks. This can create a ripple effect, inspiring others to cultivate a more positive and nurturing relationship with themselves.

In addition to setting boundaries and practicing self-compassion, modeling self-care also involves engaging in activities that promote physical and emotional well-being. This may include regular exercise, nutritious eating, adequate sleep, and stress-reducing activities such as yoga or meditation. By prioritizing these practices in their own lives, individuals can demonstrate the importance of taking care of one's physical health and emotional well-being. This can serve as a powerful example for others, inspiring them to adopt similar self-care practices in their own lives.

Furthermore, modeling self-care involves seeking support and resources to enhance one's well-being. This may include seeking therapy or counseling, participating in support groups, or accessing other resources that can provide guidance and assistance. By demonstrating a willingness to seek help when needed, individuals can show others that it is not a sign of weakness but a sign of strength to prioritize one's mental health and well-being. This can help reduce the stigma surrounding mental health issues and encourage others to seek the support they need to thrive. By setting boundaries, practicing self-compassion, engaging in healthy practices, and seeking support, individuals can demonstrate the importance of prioritizing their own needs and nurturing themselves in a holistic manner. By modeling healthy self-care practices, individuals can inspire others to take care of themselves and create a more supportive and nurturing community for all.

Chapter 10: Celebrating Parenting

- Finding Joy in Parenthood

Parenthood is undoubtedly one of the most challenging yet rewarding experiences a person can have in their lifetime. From the moment a child is born, parents are faced with a myriad of responsibilities, worries, and sacrifices. However, amidst all the chaos and exhaustion that often comes with raising children, there is also an abundance of joy to be found. Finding joy in parenthood is not always easy, but with the right mindset and approach, it is certainly possible.

One of the key ways to find joy in parenthood is by embracing the small moments and cherishing the simple joys that come with raising a child. From a baby's first smile to a toddler's infectious laughter, these moments may seem fleeting, but they are what make all the hard work and sacrifices worthwhile. By slowing down and savoring these moments, parents can find happiness in the everyday tasks of parenting.

Another way to find joy in parenthood is by cultivating a strong bond with your child. Building a loving and supportive relationship with your child can bring immense joy and fulfillment to both parties. Taking the time to truly connect with your child, to listen to their thoughts and feelings, and to be present in their lives can create a deep sense of satisfaction and happiness. This bond can provide a sense of purpose and meaning to parenthood, making all the challenges and struggles seem insignificant in comparison.

Additionally, finding joy in parenthood can also come from embracing the imperfections and messiness that come with raising children. Parenting is not always going to be perfect, and there will be days when things go wrong, plans fall through, and tempers flare. However, by letting go of the need for perfection and accepting that mistakes will happen, parents can find a sense of freedom and joy in the chaos. Learning to laugh at the inevitable mishaps and failures can bring a sense of lightness and levity to the parenting journey.

Furthermore, finding joy in parenthood can be enhanced by seeking out support and building a community of fellow parents. Connecting with other parents who are going through similar experiences can provide a source of comfort and understanding. Sharing stories, advice, and laughter with others can help alleviate the sense of isolation and overwhelm that can sometimes accompany parenthood. By forming a support network, parents can find joy in the shared experiences and camaraderie that come with raising children. By focusing on the small moments, building a strong bond with your child, embracing imperfection, and seeking out support, parents can cultivate a sense of happiness and fulfillment in their role as caregivers. Parenthood may be challenging, but it is also a source of immense joy and love that can enrich and transform your life in ways you never thought possible.

- Recognizing Achievements and Milestones

Recognizing achievements and milestones is an essential component of any successful organization. By acknowledging the hard work and dedication of individuals or teams, leaders can foster a culture of appreciation and motivation that drives continued success. Whether it's a small personal goal reached or a major project completed, celebrating these accomplishments provides a sense of validation and pride that inspires others to strive for their own achievements.

In the workplace, recognizing achievements can take many forms. From a simple thank you note to a public announcement or formal award ceremony, there are countless ways to show appreciation for a job well done. One effective method is to establish a recognition program that highlights specific milestones or goals that align with the organization's values and objectives. This can include recognizing employees who consistently go above and beyond in their role, or teams that collaboratively achieve significant results.

It's important to remember that recognition should be genuine and personalized. Generic praise or rewards that don't reflect the individual's or team's unique contributions can feel insincere and may even have the opposite effect of demotivating rather than inspiring. Taking the time to understand what achievements are meaningful to each person and tailoring recognition accordingly shows that their efforts are truly valued and appreciated.

In addition to recognizing individual achievements, it's also important to celebrate milestones that mark significant progress or success for the organization as a whole. This could be the completion of a major project, reaching a revenue target, or even an anniversary that signifies years of dedication and growth. By acknowledging these milestones, leaders can reinforce the organization's sense of purpose and shared accomplishments, creating a sense of unity and pride among employees.

Furthermore, recognizing achievements and milestones can have a ripple effect throughout the organization. When employees see their colleagues being celebrated for their hard work, they are more likely to feel inspired to push themselves to reach their own goals. This creates a positive feedback loop that drives continuous improvement and innovation, as individuals and teams strive to outdo themselves and contribute to the overall success of the organization.

Ultimately, recognizing achievements and milestones is not just a feel-good gesture – it's a strategic tool for driving performance and success. When employees feel valued and appreciated for their efforts, they are more engaged, motivated, and loyal to the organization. This in turn leads to higher levels of productivity, creativity, and collaboration, all of which are key ingredients for sustained growth and success. By making recognition a priority and integrating it into the organization's culture, leaders can create a positive and supportive work environment where individuals and teams are empowered to achieve their full potential.

- Embracing the Role of a Parent

Embracing the role of a parent is a multifaceted and rewarding journey that requires dedication, patience, and love. As parents, we are entrusted with the immense responsibility of nurturing and guiding our children as they navigate through the various stages of life. This role is not without its challenges, but with the right mindset and approach, we can create a nurturing and supportive environment that fosters growth and development.

One of the most important aspects of embracing the role of a parent is recognizing the profound impact that we have on our children's lives. From the moment they are born, children look to their parents for love, support, and guidance. As parents, we have the power to shape our children's beliefs, values, and behaviors through our words and actions. This immense influence can be both intimidating and empowering, but by approaching parenthood with intention and mindfulness, we can create a positive and nurturing environment that sets our children up for success.

In order to effectively embrace the role of a parent, it is important to create a strong bond with our children based on trust, respect, and communication. Building a positive relationship with our children is essential for fostering their emotional and social development. By listening to our children, showing empathy, and offering support, we can create a safe and loving environment where they feel valued and understood. This open line of communication is crucial for addressing their needs and concerns, and for helping them navigate the challenges that they may face.

Another important aspect of embracing the role of a parent is setting clear boundaries and expectations for our children. Boundaries provide children with a sense of security and structure, and help them understand what is expected of them. By establishing consistent rules and consequences, we can teach our children about responsibility, accountability, and self-discipline. It is important to remember that setting boundaries is not about being authoritarian or controlling, but rather about creating a safe and supportive environment where children can learn and grow.

In addition to setting boundaries, it is important for parents to be actively involved in their children's lives and to provide them with opportunities for growth and exploration. This can include participating in activities together, engaging in meaningful conversations, and supporting their interests and passions. By showing an interest in our children's lives and actively engaging with them, we can strengthen our bond and create lasting memories that they will cherish for years to come.

As parents, it is also important to practice self-care and to prioritize our own well-being. Parenting can be emotionally and physically draining, and it is important to take time for ourselves to recharge and rejuvenate. By taking care of ourselves, we can be better equipped to handle the challenges of parenthood and to be present and engaged with our children. This can include engaging in hobbies and activities that bring us joy, seeking support from friends and family, and practicing mindfulness and self-reflection. By recognizing the profound impact that we have on our children's lives, building a strong bond based on trust and communication, setting clear boundaries and expectations, being actively involved in our children's lives, and prioritizing our own well-being, we can create a positive and nurturing environment that fosters growth and development. Parenting is not without its challenges, but with the right mindset and approach, we can navigate this journey with grace and compassion, and create lasting memories that will shape our children's lives for years to come.

Chapter 11: Navigating Parenting Styles

- Understanding Different Parenting Approaches

Parenting is a complex and multifaceted aspect of human life that has garnered much attention and research in recent years. As society evolves and changes, so too do the approaches to parenting. Understanding the different parenting approaches is crucial for parents, caregivers, and educators alike in order to support the healthy development and well-being of children.

One of the most well-known parenting approaches is authoritative parenting. This approach is characterized by setting clear and consistent boundaries for children while also being warm and nurturing. Authoritative parents encourage independence and self-discipline in their children, while also providing support and guidance. Research has shown that children raised by authoritative parents tend to have higher self-esteem, better academic performance, and lower levels of anxiety and depression. This approach is often considered the most effective and beneficial for children's overall development.

Another parenting approach that is commonly discussed is authoritarian parenting. This approach is characterized by a strict and controlling demeanor, with a focus on obedience and discipline. Authoritarian parents tend to have high expectations for their children but may not provide the emotional support and warmth that authoritative parents do. Research has shown that children raised by authoritarian parents may struggle with self-esteem issues, have difficulty expressing their emotions, and may exhibit more aggressive or rebellious behavior. While this approach may be effective in certain cultural contexts, it is generally considered less beneficial for children's overall development.

Permissive parenting is another approach that is often talked about in parenting literature. This approach is characterized by being lenient and indulgent with children, often avoiding setting firm boundaries or enforcing rules. Permissive parents tend to be highly responsive to their children's wants and desires, but may struggle with providing discipline and guidance. Research has shown that children raised by permissive parents may have difficulty regulating their emotions, struggle with impulse control, and may have lower academic performance. While permissive parenting can foster a close and supportive relationship between parent and child, it may also lead to negative outcomes if boundaries and expectations are not established.

Lastly, the uninvolved parenting approach is one in which parents are disengaged and detached from their children's lives. These parents may be neglectful, indifferent, or even hostile towards their children, leading to a lack of emotional support and guidance. Research has shown that children raised by uninvolved parents may struggle with attachment issues, have difficulty forming healthy relationships, and may exhibit behavioral problems. This approach is generally considered the least effective and beneficial for children's overall development, as children need a secure and nurturing environment in order to thrive. While each approach has its strengths and weaknesses, authoritative parenting is generally considered the most effective and beneficial for children's overall development. By setting clear and consistent boundaries, providing emotional support and guidance, and encouraging independence and self-discipline, parents can foster a positive and nurturing environment for their children to thrive. It is important for parents to be reflective and intentional in their parenting approach, taking into consideration the unique needs and personalities of their children in order to promote their growth and development.

- Finding Your Parenting Style

Parenting is a unique and deeply personal journey that every individual embarks upon when they become a parent. One of the key components of parenting is finding and developing your own parenting style. This style is a combination of your beliefs, values, and techniques that guide your interactions with your children. It is important to understand that there is no one-size-fits-all approach to parenting, and what works for one parent may not work for another. Finding your parenting style involves self-reflection, adapting to the needs of your child, and being open to changing and evolving as a parent. In this discussion, we will explore the different parenting styles, how to identify your own style, and tips for developing a positive and effective parenting approach.

There are four main parenting styles that have been identified through research and observation: authoritarian, permissive, authoritative, and uninvolved. Authoritarian parents are strict and controlling, setting high expectations for their children and enforcing rules with little explanation or flexibility. Permissive parents, on the other hand, are more lenient and indulgent, setting few rules and boundaries and allowing their children to have a lot of freedom. Authoritative parents strike a balance between control and flexibility, setting clear rules and expectations while also being responsive to their children's needs and opinions. Uninvolved parents are detached and neglectful, showing little interest in their children's lives or well-being.

To identify your own parenting style, it is important to reflect on your beliefs, values, and experiences that have shaped your approach to parenting. Consider how you were raised and how that has influenced your views on parenting. Think about your goals and expectations for your children, and how you want to interact with them on a daily basis. It may also be helpful to observe other parents and seek out advice from experts in child development to gain a better understanding of the different parenting styles.

Once you have identified your parenting style, it is important to consider how it aligns with your child's needs and temperament. Every child is unique, with their own personality, strengths, and challenges. It is important to be flexible and adaptable in your approach to parenting, tailoring your techniques to meet the needs of each individual child. This may require making adjustments to your parenting style as your child grows and develops, or as you encounter new challenges and obstacles.

One of the key principles of effective parenting is building a strong and positive relationship with your child. This involves creating a supportive and nurturing environment where your child feels loved, valued, and understood. Communication is essential in building this relationship, so be sure to listen to your child's thoughts and feelings, and provide opportunities for open and honest dialogue. Show empathy and compassion towards your child, and be willing to apologize and make amends when you make mistakes.

In addition to building a strong relationship with your child, it is important to set clear and consistent boundaries and expectations. Children thrive in a structured and predictable environment, where they know what is expected of them and what consequences they will face if they do not meet those expectations. Be firm and consistent in enforcing rules, but also be willing to explain the reasons behind them and involve your child in the decision-making process when appropriate. This will help your child understand the boundaries you have set and develop a sense of responsibility and accountability.

As a parent, it is important to practice self-care and prioritize your own well-being. Parenting can be a demanding and exhausting role, and it is easy to neglect your own needs in the midst of caring for your children. Make time for yourself to rest, relax, and recharge, whether that means taking breaks throughout the day, engaging in hobbies and activities that bring you joy, or seeking support from friends and family. Remember that you are a role model for your children, and by taking care of yourself, you are teaching them the importance of self-care and personal well-being. It involves understanding your beliefs and values, aligning your style with your child's needs, building a positive relationship with your child, setting clear boundaries and expectations, and prioritizing your own well-being. There is no one right way to parent, and what works for one family may not work for another. By being open-minded, flexible, and responsive to your child's needs, you can develop a positive and effective parenting style that nurtures your child's growth and development. Remember that parenting is a journey, and it is okay to seek help, advice, and support along the way.

- Respecting Other Parents' Choices

Respecting other parents' choices is a fundamental aspect of creating a supportive and inclusive community for families. It involves acknowledging and accepting that each parent has the right to make decisions for their child based on their own values, beliefs, and circumstances. This may include choices related to parenting styles, discipline practices, educational philosophies, and healthcare decisions. By respecting these choices, we can foster a sense of understanding, empathy, and cooperation among parents, regardless of differences in opinion or approach.

It is important to recognize that there is no one-size-fits-all approach to parenting. Every child is unique, as is every family, and what works for one family may not work for another. By respecting other parents' choices, we can create a more supportive and compassionate community where parents feel empowered to make decisions that are in the best interest of their child. This not only benefits individual families but also contributes to a more harmonious and inclusive society as a whole.

One key aspect of respecting other parents' choices is refraining from judgment or criticism. It is natural for parents to have strong opinions and feelings about how to raise their children, but it is important to remember that there is no one "right" way to parent. Instead of focusing on differences, we should strive to find common ground and mutual respect for the diversity of parenting styles and approaches that exist.

Another important aspect of respecting other parents' choices is being open to learning from each other. Just as no two children are alike, no two parents are alike either. By listening to and engaging with other parents, we can gain valuable insights and perspectives that may broaden our own understanding and enhance our own parenting practices. This spirit of openness and curiosity can lead to meaningful conversations and connections that enrich the parenting experience for everyone involved.

In addition to listening and learning from other parents, it is also important to offer support and encouragement. Parenting can be a challenging and demanding responsibility, and all parents can benefit from a sense of community and solidarity. By offering a helping hand, a sympathetic ear, or a kind word, we can create a culture of mutual support and cooperation that strengthens the bonds between parents and fosters a sense of collective responsibility for the well-being of all children.

Ultimately, respecting other parents' choices is about fostering a culture of understanding, empathy, and cooperation within the parenting community. By acknowledging and accepting the diversity of parenting styles and approaches that exist, we can create a more inclusive and supportive environment where parents feel empowered to make decisions that are in the best interest of their child. Through open-mindedness, active listening, and a spirit of collaboration, we can build stronger connections with other parents and create a healthier, more harmonious community for all families.

Chapter 12: Balancing Work and Family Life

- Managing Responsibilities

Managing responsibilities is a crucial aspect of professional and personal success. By effectively managing our responsibilities, we can achieve our goals, meet deadlines, and maintain a healthy work-life balance. In today's fast-paced world, it can be easy to become overwhelmed by the sheer number of tasks and obligations we have to juggle. However, by implementing effective strategies and techniques, we can better manage our responsibilities and reduce stress.

One key aspect of managing responsibilities is prioritization. Prioritization involves determining which tasks are most important and need to be completed first. By identifying our most important tasks and focusing on them, we can ensure that we are making progress towards our goals. One useful strategy for prioritization is the Eisenhower Matrix, which categorizes tasks into four quadrants based on their importance and urgency. By using this tool, we can quickly determine which tasks require our immediate attention and which can be deferred or delegated.

Another important aspect of managing responsibilities is time management. Time management involves allocating our time effectively to ensure that we are able to complete our tasks in a timely manner. One useful strategy for time management is the Pomodoro Technique, which involves breaking work into short intervals (typically 25 minutes) separated by short breaks. By working in focused bursts, we can increase our productivity and reduce procrastination. Additionally, using a calendar or planner to schedule our tasks and appointments can help us stay organized and on track.

Delegation is another important aspect of managing responsibilities. Delegation involves assigning tasks to others who are better suited to completing them. By delegating tasks effectively, we can free up our time to focus on more important or high-value tasks. However, delegation requires trust in the abilities of others and effective communication to ensure that tasks are completed to our satisfaction. It is important to clearly define the scope of work, set expectations, and provide any necessary resources or support to the person to whom the task is delegated.

Communication is also key to managing responsibilities effectively. Clear communication ensures that everyone involved in a project or task is on the same page and understands their roles and responsibilities. By keeping lines of communication open, we can avoid misunderstandings, confusion, and duplication of efforts. Additionally, effective communication allows us to ask for help when needed, seek clarification on tasks, and provide feedback to others. By fostering a culture of open and transparent communication, we can improve collaboration and teamwork within our organization.

Lastly, it is important to take care of ourselves while managing responsibilities. Balancing work, family, and personal responsibilities can be challenging, but self-care is essential to prevent burnout and maintain overall well-being. This can include getting enough sleep, eating healthily, exercising regularly, and taking breaks when needed. It is also important to set boundaries and learn to say no when we are feeling overwhelmed or overburdened. By prioritizing our own needs and well-being, we can better manage our responsibilities and be more effective in both our personal and professional lives.

- Making Time for Family

In today's fast-paced world, it can be challenging to find the time to spend with our families. Between work, school, extracurricular activities, and other commitments, it can feel like there are not enough hours in the day to give our loved ones the attention they deserve. However, making time for family is essential for building strong relationships, creating lasting memories, and fostering a sense of belonging and connection.

One of the first steps in making time for family is to prioritize it in our daily schedules. This may mean setting aside specific blocks of time each week dedicated solely to spending quality time with our family members. By scheduling family time in advance, we can ensure that it does not get overlooked or pushed aside by other commitments. This might involve planning weekly family dinners, organizing outings or activities, or simply setting aside time each evening to catch up and connect with one another.

Another important aspect of making time for family is to be present and engaged when we are together. In today's digital age, it can be all too easy to be distracted by our phones, computers, and other devices, even when we are in the same room as our family members. However, by putting away our devices and giving our full attention to our loved ones, we can create a more meaningful and memorable experience for everyone involved. This means actively listening to each other, participating in conversations and activities, and showing genuine interest and enthusiasm for spending time together.

Additionally, it can be helpful to involve our family members in the decision-making process when it comes to planning and organizing activities. By allowing everyone to have a say in how they want to spend their time together, we can ensure that everyone's needs and preferences are taken into account. This can help to create a more inclusive and collaborative environment and can also lead to more enjoyable and fulfilling family experiences.

In addition to scheduling specific family time and being present and engaged during these moments, it is also important to make the most of the time we have together. This may involve creating traditions, rituals, or routines that can help to strengthen family bonds and create a sense of continuity and connection. Whether it's a weekly movie night, a monthly game night, or an annual family vacation, these shared experiences can create lasting memories and help to solidify the bonds between family members.

Furthermore, it is important to recognize that quality is often more important than quantity when it comes to spending time with our families. While it may not always be possible to spend large amounts of time together due to various commitments and obligations, it is important to make the most of the time we do have. This means making an effort to be fully present, engaged, and attentive during the time we do spend with our family members, rather than simply going through the motions or going through the motions. By prioritizing family time, being present and engaged when we are together, involving our family members in the decision-making process, making the most of the time we have together, and focusing on quality over quantity, we can create meaningful and fulfilling experiences that will strengthen our relationships and bring joy and happiness to our lives.

- Finding Work-Life Balance

In today's fast-paced and interconnected world, finding a balance between work and personal life has become increasingly challenging. With the rise of technology that allows us to be constantly connected to our work, it can be difficult to switch off and focus on our personal lives. However, finding a work-life balance is essential for our overall well-being and productivity. In this article, we will discuss strategies and tips for maintaining a healthy balance between work and personal life.

One of the key factors in achieving work-life balance is setting boundaries between work and personal time. It is important to establish set work hours and stick to them as much as possible. This means avoiding the temptation to check emails or take work calls outside of these hours. By creating clear boundaries, you can ensure that you have dedicated time for both work and personal activities.

Another important aspect of achieving work-life balance is prioritizing tasks and managing your time effectively. It can be easy to get caught up in the busyness of work and feel overwhelmed by the never-ending to-do list. To avoid this, it is important to prioritize tasks based on their importance and urgency. By focusing on the most important tasks first, you can ensure that you are making progress on your work without feeling overwhelmed.

In addition to prioritizing tasks, it is also important to take breaks throughout the day to recharge and avoid burnout. Taking breaks allows your mind to rest and refocus, which can help improve your productivity and creativity. Whether it's taking a short walk outside, grabbing a coffee with a colleague, or simply stepping away from your desk for a few minutes, taking regular breaks can help you maintain a healthy work-life balance.

Finding work-life balance also involves setting realistic expectations for yourself and others. It is important to communicate your boundaries and limitations to your colleagues and supervisors, so they understand your need for work-life balance. By setting realistic expectations, you can avoid overcommitting yourself and feeling overwhelmed by your workload. It is okay to say no to additional tasks or projects if you feel that they will negatively impact your work-life balance.

Another important aspect of achieving work-life balance is taking care of your physical and mental health. It can be easy to neglect self-care when you are busy with work, but it is essential for maintaining a healthy balance between work and personal life. This includes getting enough sleep, eating a balanced diet, exercising regularly, and finding time for activities that bring you joy and relaxation. Prioritizing your health and well-being can help you feel more energized and focused, allowing you to juggle the demands of work and personal life more effectively. By setting boundaries, prioritizing tasks, taking breaks, setting realistic expectations, and taking care of your physical and mental health, you can achieve a healthy balance between work and personal life. It is important to remember that work-life balance looks different for everyone, so it is important to find what works best for you and make adjustments as needed. By making a conscious effort to maintain a healthy balance between work and personal life, you can improve your overall quality of life and be more successful in both areas.

Chapter 13: Sibling Relationships

- Fostering Positive Sibling Bonds

Siblings play a unique and significant role in our lives. They are our first friends, confidants, and companions. The bond between siblings is a special one that lasts a lifetime. However, fostering positive sibling bonds can sometimes be challenging, especially as children grow and develop their own personalities and interests. In this essay, we will explore the importance of fostering positive sibling bonds, as well as some practical strategies for promoting strong relationships between siblings.

First and foremost, it is important to recognize the many benefits of positive sibling relationships. Research has shown that strong sibling bonds contribute to emotional well-being, social competence, and overall life satisfaction. Siblings provide a sense of belonging, support, and connection that is unique to family relationships. They can offer comfort in times of need, celebrate achievements, and share in life's joys and sorrows. Positive sibling relationships also help children develop important social and emotional skills, such as empathy, communication, and conflict resolution.

One of the key factors in fostering positive sibling bonds is parental guidance and support. Parents play a crucial role in shaping the dynamics of sibling relationships and setting the tone for how siblings interact with one another. It is important for parents to model healthy communication, respect, and cooperation in their own relationships with their children. By demonstrating these positive behaviors, parents can help siblings learn how to navigate conflicts, resolve disagreements, and collaborate effectively.

In addition to modeling positive behaviors, parents can also create opportunities for siblings to bond and connect with one another. Family activities, such as game nights, outings, and vacations, can provide siblings with shared experiences and memories that strengthen their relationship.

Encouraging siblings to work together on projects, hobbies, or chores can also promote cooperation and teamwork. By fostering a sense of camaraderie and collaboration, parents can help siblings develop a strong bond that will carry them through the ups and downs of life.

It is also important for parents to acknowledge and validate the unique qualities and strengths of each child. Siblings are individuals with their own personalities, interests, and preferences. It is important for parents to celebrate these differences and encourage siblings to appreciate each other's strengths and talents. By fostering a sense of mutual respect and admiration, parents can help siblings see each other as allies and supporters rather than competitors or adversaries.

Another important aspect of fostering positive sibling bonds is teaching children how to manage conflicts and disagreements constructively. Siblings are bound to have disagreements and arguments from time to time, but it is essential for them to learn how to resolve conflicts peacefully and respectfully. Parents can help siblings develop these skills by teaching them techniques for active listening, expressing emotions, and finding compromises. By providing children with the tools they need to navigate conflicts effectively, parents can help siblings build a foundation of trust and understanding in their relationship. By recognizing the importance of sibling relationships, modeling positive behaviors, creating opportunities for bonding, acknowledging individual strengths, and teaching conflict resolution skills, parents can help siblings develop a strong and lasting connection. Siblings have the potential to be each other's greatest allies, supporters, and friends. By fostering positive sibling bonds, parents can help children build a foundation of love, respect, and understanding that will last a lifetime.

- Managing Sibling Rivalry

Sibling rivalry is a common phenomenon that occurs in many households, often leading to conflicts and tension between brothers and sisters. It is a natural part of growing up and can have both positive and negative effects on the development of children. In order to effectively manage sibling rivalry, parents and caregivers must understand the underlying causes and implement strategies to promote harmony and cooperation among siblings.

One of the main causes of sibling rivalry is competition for attention and resources. Children may feel jealous or resentful towards their siblings if they perceive that one is receiving more love, affection, or privileges than the other. This can lead to feelings of insecurity and a desire to "compete" for the parent's approval and affection. In many cases, siblings may also engage in rivalry in order to establish their own identity and differentiate themselves from their brothers or sisters.

Another common cause of sibling rivalry is differences in temperament and personality. Children may have different interests, strengths, and weaknesses, which can lead to conflicts and disagreements. Siblings may also have different communication styles and ways of expressing themselves, which can exacerbate tensions and misunderstandings. Additionally, children who are close in age may feel a sense of competition or comparison with one another, leading to rivalry and conflicts.

In order to manage sibling rivalry effectively, parents and caregivers must first recognize that it is a normal part of sibling relationships and not something to be ignored or dismissed. By acknowledging and addressing the underlying causes of rivalry, caregivers can help children navigate their feelings and develop healthier ways of interacting with their siblings. It is important for parents to model positive communication and conflict resolution skills, as children often learn how to manage their relationships by observing the behavior of adults in their lives.

One strategy for managing sibling rivalry is to establish clear and consistent rules and boundaries within the household. By setting expectations for behavior and enforcing consequences for negative actions, parents can create a sense of fairness and accountability among siblings. It is important for parents to treat each child as an individual and avoid playing favorites, as this can fuel feelings of resentment and jealousy. By creating a harmonious and structured environment, parents can help siblings learn how to share, cooperate, and resolve conflicts in a healthy and constructive manner.

Additionally, parents can encourage positive sibling relationships by fostering a sense of teamwork and collaboration among siblings. By promoting activities that require cooperation and mutual support, such as team sports or group projects, parents can help children learn how to work together as a team and appreciate each other's strengths and contributions. It is important for parents to celebrate and acknowledge the unique qualities and accomplishments of each child, while also encouraging empathy and understanding towards siblings. By promoting a sense of unity and solidarity within the family, parents can help siblings develop stronger bonds and reduce feelings of rivalry and competition. By addressing the underlying causes of rivalry and implementing strategies to promote harmony and cooperation among siblings, parents can help children navigate their relationships in a healthy and constructive manner. It is important for parents to model positive behavior and provide consistent guidance and support to help siblings develop empathy, communication skills, and conflict resolution strategies. By fostering a sense of unity and collaboration within the family, parents can create a supportive and nurturing environment in which siblings can thrive and grow together.

- Encouraging Cooperation and Empathy

In today's interconnected world, the ability to cooperate and show empathy towards others is more important than ever. Whether it's in the workplace, in social settings, or on a global scale, the ability to work together and understand the perspectives of others can lead to more positive outcomes and a more harmonious society. Encouraging cooperation and empathy can bring people together, build stronger relationships, and create a more inclusive and compassionate world.

Cooperation is essential for achieving common goals and solving complex problems. By working together, individuals can combine their skills, knowledge, and resources to achieve more than they could on their own. In the workplace, cooperation among team members can lead to increased productivity, improved efficiency, and better outcomes for the organization as a whole. By encouraging cooperation, leaders can create a culture of collaboration and teamwork that can drive innovation and success.

Empathy is equally important for building strong relationships and fostering understanding among individuals. Empathy is the ability to understand and share the feelings of others, to put oneself in someone else's shoes and see the world from their perspective. By showing empathy towards others, we can build trust, create connections, and foster a sense of community and belonging. Empathy can help to bridge the gap between people of different backgrounds, cultures, and beliefs, and promote mutual respect and understanding.

Encouraging cooperation and empathy requires a conscious effort on the part of individuals, leaders, and organizations. It involves actively listening to others, seeking to understand their perspectives, and showing empathy towards their experiences and feelings. It also involves being willing to collaborate with others, to work towards common goals, and to support one another in times of need. By fostering a culture of cooperation and empathy, we can create a more compassionate and inclusive society where people feel valued, respected, and supported.

There are many ways to encourage cooperation and empathy in our daily lives. One way is to practice active listening, which involves truly hearing what others have to say, without judgment or interruption. By listening attentively to others, we can better understand their perspectives and show that we value their thoughts and feelings. Another way to promote cooperation and empathy is to engage in open and honest communication, to share our own thoughts and feelings, and to encourage others to do the same. By being transparent and vulnerable, we can build trust and create deeper connections with others.

In the workplace, leaders can play a crucial role in promoting cooperation and empathy among team members. By setting a positive example through their own actions and behaviors, leaders can inspire others to work together towards common goals and to show empathy towards their colleagues. Leaders can also create opportunities for team members to collaborate on projects, share ideas, and support one another in achieving their objectives. By fostering a culture of cooperation and empathy, leaders can create a more engaged and motivated workforce that is committed to success.

On a larger scale, encouraging cooperation and empathy can have far-reaching benefits for society as a whole. By coming together to address common challenges, such as poverty, inequality, and climate change, we can create a more sustainable and equitable world for future generations. By showing empathy towards those who are less fortunate or marginalized, we can create a more compassionate and inclusive society where everyone has the opportunity to thrive. By working together towards a common purpose, we can build a brighter future for all. By working together, showing empathy towards others, and building strong relationships, we can create a more inclusive and equitable society where everyone feels valued and supported. By fostering a culture of cooperation and empathy in our daily lives, in the workplace, and on a global scale, we can build a brighter future for ourselves and for future generations. Let us all strive to be more cooperative, empathetic, and understanding towards one another, and together, we can create a better world for all.

Chapter 14: Technology and Parenting

- Setting Screen Time Limits

In today's digital age, screen time has become a pervasive aspect of our daily lives. From smartphones to tablets to computers, we are constantly surrounded by screens and the temptation to constantly be connected to technology. While technology has its benefits and can enhance our lives in many ways, it is important to recognize the potential negative effects of excessive screen time. This is why setting screen time limits is crucial for maintaining a healthy balance between technology use and other aspects of our lives.

Setting screen time limits is not about completely eliminating technology from our lives, but rather about being mindful of how much time we spend in front of screens and ensuring that we are not neglecting other important aspects of our lives. Excessive screen time has been linked to a variety of negative outcomes, including poor sleep, eye strain, decreased physical activity, and even mental health issues such as anxiety and depression. By setting limits on how much time we spend using screens, we can help mitigate these potential negative effects and ensure that we are living a balanced and healthy lifestyle.

When it comes to setting screen time limits, it is important to establish clear and consistent rules for both children and adults. For children, screen time limits are particularly important as excessive screen time can interfere with their development and overall well-being. The American Academy of Pediatrics recommends that children aged 2-5 should have no more than 1 hour of screen time per day, while older children and teenagers should have consistent limits on the amount of time they spend using screens. By setting these limits early on and enforcing them consistently, parents can help their children develop healthy screen time habits that will serve them well in the long run.

For adults, setting screen time limits can also be beneficial for maintaining a healthy work-life balance and ensuring that we are not constantly tethered to our devices. With the rise of remote work and the blurred line between work and personal life, it can be easy to fall into the trap of constantly checking emails and notifications on our devices. By setting limits on when and how much time we spend on screens, we can create boundaries that allow us to disconnect and focus on other aspects of our lives, such as spending time with loved ones, engaging in hobbies, and getting regular exercise.

In addition to setting screen time limits, it is also important to consider the quality of screen time that we engage in. Not all screen time is created equal, and spending hours scrolling mindlessly through social media or watching endless hours of television can be just as detrimental as spending excessive time on work-related tasks. Instead, it is important to prioritize screen time that is productive, engaging, and enhances our overall well-being. This could include activities such as reading e-books, engaging in online courses, or connecting with loved ones through video calls. By focusing on quality screen time, we can make the most of our digital devices while minimizing the potential negative effects of excessive screen time. By establishing clear and consistent rules for both children and adults, we can help mitigate the negative effects of excessive screen time and ensure that we are living a balanced and healthy lifestyle. By prioritizing quality screen time and being mindful of how much time we spend in front of screens, we can make the most of our digital devices while also engaging in other important activities that contribute to our overall well-being.

- Monitoring Online Activities

In today's digital age, monitoring online activities has become a crucial aspect of both personal and professional life. With the increasing prevalence of cyber threats and the growing importance of online security, it is more important than ever to stay vigilant and proactive in monitoring one's online activities. Whether it be for protecting personal information from hackers or ensuring compliance with company policies, monitoring online activities is essential for maintaining a safe and secure online environment.

One of the key reasons for monitoring online activities is to protect privacy and security. In an age where personal information is constantly being collected and shared online, it is important to take measures to safeguard one's privacy. By monitoring online activities, individuals can identify potential threats such as phishing scams, malware, or unauthorized access to personal information. This proactive approach can help prevent identity theft and other forms of cyber fraud, ensuring that sensitive information remains confidential and secure.

Monitoring online activities is also important for maintaining compliance with company policies and regulations. Many organizations have strict guidelines regarding internet usage and online behavior, especially when accessing company networks or using company-owned devices. By monitoring online activities, employers can ensure that employees are adhering to these policies and are not engaging in any activities that could put the organization at risk. This could include monitoring emails, website visits, and social media usage to ensure that employees are not disclosing confidential information or engaging in inappropriate behavior online.

Additionally, monitoring online activities can help detect and prevent cyber threats before they escalate. With the rise of cyber attacks and data breaches, it is critical for individuals and organizations to stay vigilant and proactive in monitoring their online activities. By monitoring for suspicious activities or unusual behavior, individuals can identify potential threats early on and take the necessary steps to mitigate them. This could include installing antivirus software, updating security settings, or contacting the appropriate authorities for assistance. Whether it be for protecting privacy, ensuring compliance with company policies, or detecting and preventing cyber threats, monitoring online activities is essential for safeguarding personal and sensitive information. By staying vigilant and proactive in monitoring online activities, individuals and organizations can protect themselves from cyber threats and ensure a safe and secure online experience.

- Teaching Digital Literacy

Digital literacy is a crucial skill that encompasses the ability to access, evaluate, create, and communicate information effectively using technology. In today's increasingly digital world, this skill is more important than ever before. As educators, it is our responsibility to teach our students how to navigate the digital landscape safely and effectively. By incorporating digital literacy into our curriculum, we can help our students become more informed and responsible digital citizens.

Teaching digital literacy begins with helping students understand the basic concepts of digital technology. This includes teaching them how to use common tools such as computers, smartphones, and the internet. Students should also learn about the importance of digital security and privacy, as well as how to protect themselves from online threats such as cyberbullying and phishing scams. By starting with these foundational concepts, students can build a strong understanding of how digital technology works and how to use it safely and effectively.

One of the key aspects of teaching digital literacy is helping students develop critical thinking skills. In today's digital age, information is more abundant than ever before, but not all of it is reliable or accurate. It is important for students to be able to evaluate the information they encounter online and determine its credibility. By teaching students how to critically analyze information and sources, we can help them become more discerning consumers of information and less susceptible to misinformation and fake news.

In addition to teaching students how to evaluate information, we should also teach them how to create and communicate information effectively using digital tools. This includes teaching students how to write and edit digital documents, create multimedia presentations, and collaborate with others online. By giving students the skills to create and share their own digital content, we can empower them to become active contributors to the digital world and to engage with others in meaningful ways.

Another important aspect of teaching digital literacy is helping students understand the ethical implications of their online behavior. This includes teaching students about issues such as online privacy, copyright infringement, and digital etiquette. By educating students about these topics, we can help them become more responsible digital citizens who respect the rights and privacy of others and use technology in a thoughtful and ethical manner. By helping students develop the skills to access, evaluate, create, and communicate information effectively using technology, we can empower them to navigate the digital landscape with confidence and responsibility. As educators, it is our responsibility to equip our students with the knowledge and skills they need to thrive in an increasingly digital world. By incorporating digital literacy into our curriculum, we can help our students become informed, engaged, and ethical digital citizens who are prepared to succeed in the 21st century.

Chapter 15: Single Parenting

- Coping with Challenges

Coping with challenges is an essential skill that everyone must develop in order to thrive in today's fast-paced and constantly evolving world. Whether it's a personal setback, a professional obstacle, or a global crisis, we all face challenges at some point in our lives. The key to coping with these challenges is having the right mindset and strategies to navigate through difficult times and come out stronger on the other side.

One of the first steps in coping with challenges is acknowledging and accepting the situation for what it is. It's important to recognize that challenges are a normal part of life and that it's okay to feel overwhelmed or upset when faced with adversity. By acknowledging and accepting the challenge, you can start to take control of the situation and think more clearly about how to address it.

Once you have accepted the challenge, the next step is to identify the specific issues or obstacles that need to be addressed. This may involve breaking down the challenge into smaller, more manageable tasks, or seeking support and advice from others who have faced similar challenges. By breaking down the challenge into smaller parts, you can create a plan of action that will help you navigate through the difficulties and overcome the obstacles in your path.

Another important aspect of coping with challenges is maintaining a positive attitude and mindset. It's easy to become discouraged or lose motivation when facing a difficult situation, but staying positive and focused on finding solutions can help you persevere through tough times. Surrounding yourself with supportive and encouraging people, practicing self-care and mindfulness techniques, and setting realistic goals can all help you maintain a positive attitude and mindset in the face of adversity.

It's also important to remember that coping with challenges is not a solo journey - it's okay to ask for help and support when needed. Whether it's reaching out to friends and family for emotional support, seeking guidance from a mentor or therapist, or joining a support group to connect with others facing similar challenges, having a strong support system can make a big difference in how you cope with difficult situations. Remember, it's not a sign of weakness to ask for help - in fact, it's a sign of strength to recognize when you need support and reach out for it.

In addition to seeking support from others, developing healthy coping mechanisms and self-care practices can also help you navigate through challenges more effectively. This can include engaging in activities that bring you joy and relaxation, such as exercise, meditation, hobbies, or spending time in nature. Taking care of your physical, mental, and emotional well-being is essential when facing challenges, as it can help you stay resilient and better equipped to handle difficult situations.

Lastly, it's important to remember that coping with challenges is a process that takes time and patience. It's okay to have setbacks or moments of doubt along the way - what's important is how you respond to these challenges and continue to move forward despite the obstacles in your path. By staying focused, positive, and resilient, you can develop the necessary skills and strategies to cope with challenges and emerge stronger and more resilient on the other side. Remember, challenges are an opportunity for growth and learning - embrace them as a chance to strengthen your resilience and discover your inner strength.

- Building a Support Network

Building a support network is a vital component of success in both personal and professional endeavors. A support network is essentially a group of individuals who provide emotional, practical, and sometimes financial support to an individual in need. This network can consist of family, friends, colleagues, mentors, and even online communities. Having a strong support network can help individuals navigate challenges, overcome obstacles, and achieve their goals more effectively.

One of the key benefits of having a support network is the emotional support it provides. Life can be unpredictable and challenging, and having a group of people who are there to listen, offer advice, and provide encouragement can make a world of difference. Whether you are dealing with a tough work situation, going through a personal crisis, or simply feeling overwhelmed, having people you can turn to for support can help you cope with difficult emotions and gain perspective on your situation.

In addition to emotional support, a strong support network can also provide practical assistance. This can include anything from helping with childcare or household chores to offering professional advice or connections. For example, if you are starting a new business, having a mentor or experienced entrepreneur in your support network can provide valuable guidance and insights. If you are going through a medical crisis, having friends or family members who can help drive you to appointments or cook meals can be a lifesaver.

Moreover, building a support network can also lead to increased opportunities for personal and professional growth. By surrounding yourself with positive and motivated individuals, you are more likely to be inspired to set and achieve ambitious goals. Your support network can also offer feedback on your ideas, introduce you to new opportunities, and hold you accountable for your actions. This can be especially valuable if you tend to procrastinate or doubt your abilities, as your support network can help you stay focused and confident in your pursuits.

When it comes to building a support network, it is important to be intentional and strategic in your approach. Start by identifying the people in your life who are already supportive and reliable. These could be family members, close friends, colleagues, or mentors. Reach out to these individuals and express your gratitude for their support, as well as your desire to deepen and strengthen your relationship with them. Be open and honest about your needs and goals, and ask for their input and advice on how to best build a support network that will help you thrive.

In addition to cultivating existing relationships, it is also important to actively seek out new connections and opportunities to expand your support network.

This can involve joining professional organizations, attending networking events, or participating in online communities that align with your interests and goals. Look for individuals who share your values and aspirations, and who can offer diverse perspectives and experiences. Building a diverse support network can help you gain new insights, challenge your assumptions, and broaden your horizons. By surrounding yourself with positive, reliable, and motivated individuals, you can navigate life's challenges more effectively, seize new opportunities for growth and development, and ultimately achieve your goals. Remember to be intentional and strategic in cultivating your support network, and to nurture your relationships with care and gratitude. With a strong support network by your side, you can overcome obstacles, reach new heights, and live a more fulfilling and meaningful life.

- Thriving as a Single Parent

Being a single parent can be a challenging and overwhelming experience, but with the right mindset and support system, it is possible to thrive in this role. Single parents often face unique challenges, such as balancing work and parenting responsibilities, managing finances on a single income, and dealing with the emotional strain of raising a child alone. However, there are also many benefits to being a single parent, such as developing a strong bond with your child, gaining a sense of independence and self-reliance, and setting a positive example for your child by showing them how to overcome adversity.

One of the most important keys to thriving as a single parent is to prioritize self-care and seek support when needed. Taking care of yourself physically, emotionally, and mentally is essential to being able to effectively care for your child. This means making time for yourself to relax, recharge, and engage in activities that bring you joy and fulfillment. It also means reaching out to friends, family members, or support groups for help when you need it, whether that means asking for assistance with childcare, seeking out advice on parenting issues, or simply having someone to talk to when you're feeling overwhelmed.

Another important aspect of thriving as a single parent is to establish a routine and set boundaries to help manage your time and energy effectively. Creating a schedule that works for both you and your child can help reduce stress and increase productivity. This might include setting aside specific times for work, household chores, and quality time with your child, as well as making time for activities that allow you to relax and unwind. Setting boundaries with your child, such as establishing rules and consequences for behavior, can also help maintain a sense of order and stability in your home.

Financial management is another key factor in thriving as a single parent. Living on a single income can be challenging, but with careful planning and budgeting, it is possible to provide for your child's needs and secure a stable financial future. This might involve prioritizing essential expenses such as food, housing, and healthcare, as well as finding ways to cut costs and save money where possible. Seeking out financial assistance programs or resources for single parents can also help alleviate financial stress and provide additional support.

Building a strong support network is crucial for thriving as a single parent. Surrounding yourself with friends, family members, and other parents who understand and support your situation can provide valuable encouragement, advice, and practical assistance. This might include attending support groups for single parents, participating in community activities or events, or simply reaching out to friends for a listening ear or a helping hand. Building strong relationships with your child's teachers, caregivers, and other individuals in your community can also create a support system that can help you navigate the challenges of single parenting.

Emotional resilience is another key factor in thriving as a single parent. Raising a child alone can be emotionally taxing, and it is important to cultivate coping strategies and techniques to help you manage stress, anxiety, and other negative emotions. This might involve practicing mindfulness and self-care activities such as meditation, yoga, or journaling, as well as seeking therapy or counseling to work through any underlying issues or traumas. Developing a positive mindset and focusing on gratitude, resilience, and self-compassion can also help boost your emotional well-being and create a sense of inner strength and confidence. By prioritizing self-care, establishing routines and boundaries, managing finances effectively, building a strong support network, and cultivating emotional resilience, you can not only survive but thrive in your role as a single parent. Remember that you are not alone and that there are resources and people available to help you navigate the challenges of single parenting. By taking care of yourself, seeking support when needed, and being proactive in managing your time, finances, and emotions, you can create a happy, healthy, and fulfilling life for both you and your child.

Chapter 16: Blended Families

- Navigating Complex Family Dynamics

Family dynamics can be incredibly complex and multifaceted, encompassing a wide range of relationships, personalities, and emotions. Navigating these dynamics can be challenging and sometimes overwhelming, but it is essential to foster healthy and positive relationships within the family unit. Whether dealing with conflicts between siblings, disagreements between parents and children, or issues with extended family members, understanding and effectively communicating within the family is key to maintaining harmony and cohesion.

One of the first steps in navigating complex family dynamics is to acknowledge and accept the unique characteristics and individual differences within the family. Each family member brings their own set of values, beliefs, and experiences to the table, which can often lead to disagreements or misunderstandings. By recognizing and respecting these differences, family members can begin to appreciate each other's perspectives and work towards finding common ground.

Effective communication is also crucial when dealing with complex family dynamics. Open and honest communication can help to address underlying issues, express emotions, and resolve conflicts in a constructive manner. It is important for family members to listen to each other without judgment, validate each other's feelings, and communicate their own needs and boundaries clearly. By fostering an environment of open communication, family members can build trust, empathy, and understanding with one another.

Setting boundaries and establishing clear expectations within the family can also help to navigate complex family dynamics. Boundaries help to define personal space, responsibilities, and limits within relationships, and they are essential for maintaining respect and autonomy among family members. By establishing clear boundaries and expectations, family members can prevent misunderstandings, conflicts, and power struggles, and create a sense of safety and security within the family unit.

Seeking support from outside resources can also be beneficial when navigating complex family dynamics. Family therapy, counseling, or mediation can provide a neutral and safe space for family members to explore their relationships, work through conflicts, and develop effective communication skills. Additionally, reaching out to trusted friends, mentors, or community support groups can offer valuable perspective, guidance, and encouragement during challenging times.

Ultimately, navigating complex family dynamics requires patience, understanding, and a willingness to work towards positive change and growth within the family. By acknowledging and accepting differences, promoting open communication, setting boundaries, and seeking outside support when needed, family members can strengthen their relationships, build resilience, and create a supportive and loving family environment. While it may not always be easy, navigating complex family dynamics can lead to greater understanding, connection, and harmony within the family unit.

- Creating Harmony in Blended Families

Blended families are becoming increasingly common in today's society, as the divorce rate continues to rise and people find love and happiness with new partners. However, blending two families together can be a challenging and complex process, as different family dynamics, values, and traditions come into play. Creating harmony in blended families requires open communication, mutual respect, and a willingness to work together to create a sense of unity and cohesion.

One of the key factors in creating harmony in blended families is communication. It is essential for all family members to communicate openly and honestly with each other about their thoughts, feelings, and concerns. This includes discussing boundaries, rules, and expectations within the new family unit, as well as addressing any conflicts or issues that may arise. By fostering open communication, family members can better understand each other's perspectives and work together to find solutions to any problems that may arise.

Another important aspect of creating harmony in blended families is mutual respect. It is crucial for all family members to respect each other's differences, opinions, and boundaries. This includes respecting each other's parenting styles, personal space, and cultural or religious beliefs. By demonstrating respect towards one another, family members can build trust and create a positive and supportive environment within the blended family.

In addition to communication and respect, it is essential for family members in blended families to work together as a team to create a sense of unity and cohesion. This includes participating in family activities together, creating new traditions and rituals as a blended family, and supporting one another through life's ups and downs. By working together as a team, family members can strengthen their bonds and create a sense of belonging and connection within the blended family.

Creating harmony in blended families also requires flexibility and compromise. It is important for family members to be willing to adapt to new challenges and changes that may arise as the family unit evolves over time. This may include adjusting schedules, sharing resources, and finding ways to balance the needs and interests of all family members. By being flexible and willing to compromise, family members can navigate the complexities of blending two families together more effectively.

Ultimately, creating harmony in blended families requires patience, understanding, and a commitment to working together as a team. It is important for family members to acknowledge that blending two families together is a process that takes time and effort, but with dedication and perseverance, a sense of harmony and unity can be achieved. By fostering open communication, mutual respect, and a willingness to work together, blended families can create a positive and supportive environment where all family members can thrive and grow together.

- Building Relationships with Stepchildren

Building relationships with stepchildren can be a complex and challenging process, but it is also incredibly rewarding when approached with patience, understanding, and empathy. Stepfamilies are becoming increasingly common in today's society, and navigating the dynamics of blended families requires a unique set of skills and strategies. In this article, we will explore the importance of building positive relationships with stepchildren, as well as practical tips and techniques for fostering strong connections and creating a sense of unity within the family unit.

One of the first steps in building relationships with stepchildren is to establish open and honest communication. It is important for both stepparents and stepchildren to communicate their feelings, concerns, and expectations in a respectful and constructive manner. This can help to build trust and understanding between all family members and create a foundation for a strong and healthy relationship. Stepparents should make an effort to listen to their stepchildren and validate their emotions, even if they may not always agree with them.

Another key aspect of building relationships with stepchildren is to show genuine interest in their lives and activities. Stepparents can engage in activities that their stepchildren enjoy, such as playing sports, watching movies, or simply having conversations about their interests and hobbies. By showing a genuine interest in their stepchildren's lives, stepparents can demonstrate that they care about their well-being and are invested in building a meaningful and positive relationship with them.

It is also important for stepparents to be patient and understanding when building relationships with stepchildren. It takes time for relationships to develop and grow, and it is normal for there to be challenges and setbacks along the way. Stepparents should be patient and understanding when their stepchildren are resistant or hesitant to open up to them, and should not take it personally. Building relationships with stepchildren is a gradual process that requires mutual respect, trust, and understanding.

In addition to patience and understanding, it is important for stepparents to establish boundaries and rules within the family unit. Creating a sense of structure and consistency can help to maintain harmony and stability within the household and can help to build trust and respect between all family members. Stepparents should work with their partner to establish clear guidelines and expectations for behavior, and should enforce these rules consistently and fairly.

Another important aspect of building relationships with stepchildren is to avoid comparing them to biological children or putting unrealistic expectations on them. Each child is unique and has their own individual strengths and weaknesses, and it is important for stepparents to appreciate and celebrate these differences. Stepparents should avoid making negative comparisons between stepchildren and biological children, as this can create feelings of resentment and insecurity.

It is also important for stepparents to be supportive and nurturing towards their stepchildren, particularly during times of transition or change. Stepparents can provide emotional support and reassurance to their stepchildren, as well as help them to navigate the challenges and difficulties of blending families. By being a positive and supportive presence in their stepchildren's lives, stepparents can help to foster a sense of security and belonging within the family unit.

Building relationships with stepchildren requires a great deal of patience, understanding, and empathy. It is a gradual process that requires time, effort, and commitment from both stepparents and stepchildren. By establishing open and honest communication, showing genuine interest in their lives, being patient and understanding, setting boundaries, avoiding comparisons, and providing support and nurturing, stepparents can build strong and meaningful relationships with their stepchildren. Ultimately, building positive relationships with stepchildren can create a sense of unity and belonging within the family unit, and can lead to a happier and more fulfilling family life for all involved.

Chapter 17: Parenting Through Different Stages

- Parenting Infants and Toddlers

Parenting infants and toddlers is a challenging yet rewarding experience that requires patience, dedication, and a deep understanding of child development. During the first few years of a child's life, parents play a crucial role in shaping their physical, cognitive, and emotional development. It is essential for parents to provide a safe and nurturing environment for their children to thrive and grow.

One of the key aspects of parenting infants and toddlers is establishing a strong bond through responsive and sensitive caregiving. Infants and toddlers rely on their parents for love, security, and comfort, so it is important for parents to be attuned to their child's needs and provide consistent and loving care. This can involve responding promptly to a child's cries, offering physical affection, and engaging in interactive play that promotes bonding and attachment.

In addition to meeting their child's basic needs, such as feeding, diapering, and sleeping, parents also play a crucial role in promoting their child's cognitive development. Infants and toddlers are constantly learning about the world around them, so it is important for parents to provide a stimulating environment that encourages exploration and discovery. This can involve providing age-appropriate toys, books, and activities that promote cognitive skills such as problem-solving, imaginative play, and language development.

Emotional development is another important aspect of parenting infants and toddlers. During the early years, children are developing their sense of self and learning how to regulate their emotions. Parents can support their child's emotional development by providing a secure and loving environment, modeling positive emotions and behaviors, and helping their child learn how to express their feelings in a healthy way. By acknowledging and validating their child's emotions, parents can help their child develop emotional intelligence and resilience.

It is also important for parents to establish consistent routines and boundaries to help their child feel secure and develop a sense of predictability. Infants and toddlers thrive on routine and structure, so it is helpful for parents to establish consistent meal times, nap times, and bedtimes to help their child feel safe and secure. Setting clear and age-appropriate limits can also help toddlers learn boundaries and develop self-regulation skills.

Parenting infants and toddlers can be physically and emotionally demanding, so it is important for parents to take care of themselves as well. Finding time for self-care, seeking support from friends and family, and seeking professional help when needed can all help parents navigate the challenges of parenting young children. It is also important for parents to prioritize their relationship with their partner and communicate openly and honestly about their parenting challenges and triumphs. By providing sensitive and responsive caregiving, promoting cognitive and emotional development, establishing consistent routines and boundaries, and taking care of themselves, parents can help their children thrive and grow during the early years of life. With love, support, and guidance, parents can set their children on a path towards a healthy and happy future.

- Parenting School-Aged Children

Parenting school-aged children can be a challenging and rewarding experience for parents. As children grow and develop, they go through various stages that can pose unique challenges for parents. It is important for parents to understand the developmental needs of their school-aged children in order to provide them with the support and guidance they need to thrive.

One of the key aspects of parenting school-aged children is providing them with a safe and nurturing environment in which to grow and develop. This means creating a home environment that is conducive to learning and exploration, while also setting appropriate boundaries and expectations for behavior. Parents can help their children feel secure and supported by providing them with love and attention, as well as setting clear and consistent rules and consequences.

Another important aspect of parenting school-aged children is fostering their social and emotional development. School-aged children are learning to navigate complex social relationships with their peers, and parents can play a key role in supporting them through this process. Parents can help their children develop important social skills, such as empathy, communication, and conflict resolution, by modeling positive behavior and providing opportunities for them to interact with others.

In addition to social and emotional development, parents also play a crucial role in supporting their school-aged children's academic success. Parents can support their children's learning by creating a supportive home environment that values education and encourages reading, writing, and critical thinking. By being actively involved in their children's education, parents can help them develop a love of learning and achieve academic success.

Parenting school-aged children also involves understanding and supporting their physical development. Parents can support their children's physical development by providing them with healthy meals, encouraging regular physical activity, and ensuring they get enough rest. By providing a safe and nurturing environment, supporting their social, emotional, academic, and physical development, and being actively involved in their lives, parents can help their school-aged children thrive and reach their full potential. It is important for parents to recognize the unique needs of their school-aged children and provide them with the support and guidance they need to grow and develop into happy and healthy individuals.

- Parenting Adolescents and Teens

Parenting adolescents and teens can be a challenging and rewarding experience. As young people go through this stage of development, they are faced with a multitude of changes and challenges, both physical and emotional. It is natural for parents to feel overwhelmed and unsure of how to navigate this period in their child's life. However, by understanding the unique needs and characteristics of adolescents and teens, parents can effectively support and guide them through this crucial phase.

One of the key aspects of parenting adolescents and teens is communication. As young people strive for independence and autonomy, they may be less willing to open up to their parents. It is important for parents to create a safe and supportive environment where their children feel comfortable expressing their thoughts and feelings. This can be achieved by actively listening to their children, validating their emotions, and offering guidance without judgment. By maintaining open lines of communication, parents can establish a strong foundation for healthy relationships with their adolescents and teens.

Another important factor in parenting adolescents and teens is setting boundaries and expectations. While it is essential to give young people the freedom to explore and make their own choices, parents also need to provide structure and guidance. Setting clear boundaries and expectations helps adolescents and teens understand their responsibilities and consequences of their actions. By establishing rules and limits, parents can help their children develop self-discipline and respect for authority. It is crucial for parents to be consistent and firm in enforcing boundaries, while also being flexible and understanding when necessary.

As adolescents and teens navigate the challenges of puberty and peer pressure, parents play a vital role in helping them develop a strong sense of self-esteem and self-worth. It is common for young people to experience feelings of insecurity and low self-esteem during this stage of development. Parents can support their children by providing encouragement, praise, and positive reinforcement. By acknowledging their strengths and accomplishments, parents can help boost their children's confidence and resilience. Additionally, parents can help their adolescents and teens build a positive self-image by promoting healthy habits and encouraging self-care practices.

Parenting adolescents and teens also involves addressing social and emotional issues that may arise during this period. Young people may face a range of challenges, such as peer pressure, academic stress, and mental health issues. It is crucial for parents to be aware of their children's emotional well-being and provide them with the necessary support and resources. By staying involved in their children's lives, parents can monitor their behavior and emotions, and intervene if any issues arise. It is important for parents to be empathetic and understanding, and to seek professional help if their children require additional support. By focusing on communication, setting boundaries, fostering self-esteem, and addressing social and emotional issues, parents can effectively support their children through this period of development. While challenges may arise along the way, it is essential for parents to remain consistent and supportive in their approach. By building strong and trusting relationships with their adolescents and teens, parents can help guide them towards a healthy and successful future.

Chapter 18: Parenting for the Future

- Preparing Your Child for Independence

Preparing your child for independence is a crucial aspect of parenting that requires careful planning and consideration. As parents, it is natural to want to protect and guide our children every step of the way. However, it is equally important to empower them to become self-sufficient and capable of navigating the challenges of adulthood. This process involves a combination of teaching practical skills, fostering emotional maturity, and instilling values that will serve them well as they transition into independence.

One of the first steps in preparing your child for independence is teaching them essential life skills. This includes basic tasks such as cooking, cleaning, and managing finances. By teaching your child how to prepare meals, do laundry, and budget their money, you are equipping them with the tools they need to thrive on their own. It is important to start early and gradually increase the difficulty of tasks as your child grows older. Encouraging them to take on responsibilities around the house and rewarding their efforts will help instill a sense of competence and independence.

In addition to practical skills, emotional maturity is also crucial in preparing your child for independence. This involves helping them develop self-awareness, resilience, and emotional intelligence. Encourage open communication with your child and create a safe space for them to express their feelings and thoughts. Teach them how to manage stress, cope with adversity, and make decisions with confidence. By fostering emotional maturity, you are helping your child build the resilience they will need to face challenges and setbacks with grace and determination.

Values and morals play a significant role in shaping a child's character and guiding their decisions as they navigate the complexities of adulthood. It is essential to instill in your child a strong set of values that will serve as a moral compass in times of uncertainty. Teach them the importance of honesty, integrity, and empathy. Encourage them to be compassionate, respectful, and responsible individuals. By modeling these values in your own behavior, you are setting a positive example for your child to follow.

As your child grows older and prepares to leave the nest, it is important to gradually transition from a hands-on approach to a more supportive role. Encourage your child to take on more responsibilities and make decisions independently. Provide guidance and support when needed, but avoid micromanaging or hovering over their every move. Allow them to learn from their mistakes and celebrate their successes. This will help build their confidence and sense of agency as they prepare to face the challenges of adulthood.

Ultimately, preparing your child for independence is a gradual and ongoing process that requires patience, consistency, and a supportive approach. By teaching practical skills, fostering emotional maturity, and instilling values, you are laying the foundation for your child to become a capable and independent adult. Remember to provide guidance and support along the way and trust in your child's ability to navigate the complexities of life with resilience and confidence. By preparing your child for independence, you are equipping them with the tools they need to thrive and create a fulfilling and successful life for themselves.

- Teaching Life Skills

Teaching life skills is an essential aspect of education that goes beyond traditional academic subjects. These skills are fundamental abilities that individuals need to navigate through everyday life and achieve success in various aspects of their personal and professional lives. They encompass a wide range of competencies, including communication, decision-making, problem-solving, time management, and interpersonal skills. By teaching life skills, educators can empower students to become self-sufficient, independent, and responsible individuals who can effectively handle the challenges and demands of modern society.

One of the key benefits of teaching life skills is that it helps students develop essential competencies that are not typically covered in traditional academic curricula. While subjects like math, science, and history are important for academic success, life skills are equally crucial for long-term success and well-being. For example, communication skills are essential for building relationships, resolving conflicts, and collaborating effectively with others. Decision-making skills are critical for making informed choices and evaluating options. Problem-solving skills are essential for overcoming obstacles and finding creative solutions to challenges. By teaching these skills, educators can prepare students to navigate the complexities of the real world and thrive in today's highly competitive and rapidly changing society.

Furthermore, teaching life skills helps students develop important personal qualities and values that are essential for success in all areas of life. For example, resilience and adaptability are crucial for bouncing back from setbacks and embracing change. Self-discipline and time management are essential for setting goals, staying organized, and staying focused on tasks. Empathy and teamwork are important for building strong relationships and working effectively with others. By teaching these qualities and values, educators can help students develop a strong foundation of character and integrity that will serve them well throughout their lives.

In addition, teaching life skills can have a positive impact on students' mental health and well-being. The ability to effectively manage stress, cope with emotions, and maintain a healthy work-life balance are essential components of mental health and resilience. By teaching students how to cultivate these skills, educators can help them build emotional intelligence, self-awareness, and coping strategies that will enhance their overall well-being and mental health. This can have a profound impact on students' academic performance, social relationships, and overall quality of life.

Moreover, teaching life skills can also help students develop a sense of purpose and direction in their lives. By helping students identify their values, interests, and goals, educators can empower them to make informed decisions and chart a course for their future. This can help students feel more motivated, engaged, and fulfilled as they pursue their academic and career aspirations. By teaching life skills, educators can inspire students to take ownership of their futures and become agents of positive change in their communities and the world at large. By imparting essential competencies, qualities, and values, educators can empower students to become self-sufficient, independent, and responsible individuals who can navigate through life's challenges and succeed in all areas of their lives. By fostering personal growth, mental health, and a sense of purpose, teaching life skills can have a profound impact on students' well-being, academic performance, and overall quality of life. As educators, it is our responsibility to equip students with the tools and resources they need to thrive in today's complex and fast-paced world. Through teaching life skills, we can help students realize their full potential and become active, engaged, and fulfilled members of society.

- Supporting Their Goals and Dreams

Supporting their goals and dreams is a crucial aspect of helping individuals achieve success and fulfillment in their lives. Whether it be in a personal or professional context, providing encouragement, guidance, and resources to help others pursue their aspirations is essential for fostering growth and development. By offering support, individuals are better able to overcome challenges, stay motivated, and work towards achieving their desired goals. In this way, supporting their goals and dreams not only benefits the individual but also contributes to their overall well-being and success.

One key way to support someone's goals and dreams is by actively listening to their aspirations and providing constructive feedback. By taking the time to truly understand what drives and motivates an individual, one can offer valuable insights and advice that can help guide them in the right direction. Listening attentively shows that you care about their goals and are invested in their success, which can be incredibly empowering for the individual. Additionally, providing constructive feedback can help individuals gain new perspectives and insights that they may not have considered on their own, ultimately enabling them to make more informed decisions and take positive steps towards achieving their goals.

Another important aspect of supporting someone's goals and dreams is helping them set realistic and achievable milestones. Setting clear and measurable objectives can help individuals stay focused and motivated as they work towards their ultimate goals. By breaking down larger goals into smaller, more manageable tasks, individuals can track their progress and celebrate their accomplishments along the way. This incremental approach not only helps individuals stay on track but also builds confidence and momentum as they make steady progress towards their dreams. By supporting individuals in setting realistic milestones, you can help them stay motivated and confident in their ability to succeed.

In addition to setting achievable milestones, providing resources and support can also play a crucial role in helping individuals achieve their goals and dreams. Whether it be financial assistance, access to networking opportunities, or emotional support, providing resources can help individuals overcome barriers and obstacles that may stand in the way of their success. By offering resources and support, you can empower individuals to pursue their dreams with confidence and determination, knowing that they have the necessary tools and assistance to help them succeed. Ultimately, by providing resources and support, you can help individuals overcome challenges and achieve their goals more effectively.

Furthermore, fostering a positive and supportive environment is key to helping individuals thrive and reach their goals. By creating a culture of encouragement and positivity, individuals are more likely to feel motivated and inspired to pursue their dreams. Whether it be through words of encouragement, celebrating successes, or providing a listening ear during challenging times, creating a supportive environment can help individuals feel valued and appreciated, ultimately boosting their confidence and motivation. By fostering a positive and supportive environment, you can create a space where individuals feel empowered to take risks, push themselves to new heights, and pursue their goals and dreams with passion and determination. By actively listening, providing constructive feedback, setting realistic milestones, offering resources and support, and fostering a positive and supportive environment, you can empower individuals to pursue their aspirations with confidence and determination. By offering support, guidance, and encouragement, you can help individuals overcome obstacles, stay motivated, and ultimately achieve their goals and dreams. In doing so, you not only help individuals reach their full potential but also contribute to their overall well-being and success.

Chapter 19: Practicing Self-Reflection and Growth

- Learning from Parenting Challenges

Parenting is a complex and multifaceted journey that presents a wide range of challenges for individuals. These challenges can vary greatly depending on factors such as the age of the child, their temperament, and the unique dynamics of the family. It is important for parents to approach these challenges with patience, empathy, and a willingness to learn and grow from the experiences they encounter.

One of the key lessons that parents can learn from facing challenges in parenting is the importance of adaptability and flexibility. No two children are the same, and what works for one child may not work for another. This requires parents to be open to trying new strategies and techniques, and to be willing to adjust their approach as needed. By being flexible and willing to experiment, parents can discover what works best for their child and their family, leading to more effective and harmonious parenting.

Another important lesson that parents can learn from facing challenges in parenting is the value of self-care and seeking support. Parenting can be incredibly demanding and stressful, and it is essential for parents to prioritize their own well-being in order to be able to effectively care for their children. This may involve setting boundaries, delegating tasks, and making time for activities that bring joy and relaxation. Additionally, seeking support from friends, family, or professionals can provide parents with the guidance and encouragement they need to navigate difficult situations and emotions.

Furthermore, facing challenges in parenting can provide valuable opportunities for personal growth and reflection. By examining their reactions and behaviors in challenging situations, parents can gain insight into their own strengths and weaknesses, and identify areas for improvement. This self-awareness can lead to greater emotional intelligence, empathy, and communication skills, which are essential for building strong and healthy relationships with children.

In addition to personal growth, parenting challenges can also offer important lessons in resilience and perseverance. Parenting is a long-term commitment that requires patience, determination, and the ability to bounce back from setbacks. By facing and overcoming challenges, parents can develop a sense of resilience that will serve them well in all aspects of their lives. This resilience can also be a powerful example for children, teaching them the importance of perseverance and problem-solving in the face of adversity.

Ultimately, learning from parenting challenges can lead to more fulfilling and effective parenting practices. By approaching challenges with an open mind, a willingness to learn, and a focus on personal growth and resilience, parents can develop the skills and qualities needed to navigate the ups and downs of parenting with grace and confidence. Embracing these lessons can help parents build strong, loving, and supportive relationships with their children, and create a positive and nurturing environment for their families to thrive.

- Seeking Personal Development

Personal development is a lifelong journey that involves taking conscious steps to improve oneself in various aspects of life. It encompasses a wide range of activities, such as setting goals, acquiring new skills, developing positive habits, and enhancing one's emotional intelligence. The ultimate goal of personal development is to become the best version of oneself and to achieve personal fulfillment and success.

One of the key components of personal development is self-awareness. This involves knowing oneself deeply, including one's strengths, weaknesses, values, and beliefs. Self-awareness allows individuals to understand their emotions, thoughts, and behaviors, which is essential for making positive changes in their lives. By being introspective and reflective, individuals can identify areas for improvement and take steps towards personal growth and development.

Another important aspect of personal development is goal setting. Setting clear and achievable goals helps individuals stay focused and motivated towards personal growth. Goals can be short-term or long-term, and they can be related to various aspects of life, such as career, relationships, health, and personal development. By setting specific, measurable, attainable, relevant, and time-bound (SMART) goals, individuals can track their progress and make necessary adjustments to stay on track.

In addition to setting goals, acquiring new skills is a crucial part of personal development. Whether it's learning a new language, improving communication skills, or developing technical expertise, acquiring new skills can help individuals grow personally and professionally. Continuous learning and skill development are essential in today's fast-paced and ever-changing world, where new technologies and trends emerge constantly. By staying curious and open to learning, individuals can adapt to new challenges and opportunities in their personal and professional lives.

Developing positive habits is another key aspect of personal development. Habits are behaviors that are ingrained in individuals' daily routines, and they play a significant role in shaping their lives. By developing positive habits, such as exercising regularly, practicing mindfulness, and maintaining a healthy diet, individuals can improve their overall well-being and achieve personal growth. It takes time and effort to develop new habits, but with consistency and determination, individuals can create lasting changes that have a positive impact on their lives.

Emotional intelligence, or EQ, is also an essential component of personal development. EQ refers to individuals' ability to recognize, understand, and manage their own emotions, as well as the emotions of others. It involves skills such as self-awareness, self-regulation, empathy, and social skills, which are crucial for building strong relationships and navigating social interactions effectively. By developing emotional intelligence, individuals can improve their communication, decision-making, and problem-solving skills, which are essential for personal and professional success. By taking conscious steps to improve oneself in various aspects of life, individuals can achieve personal fulfillment, success, and well-being. Personal development requires commitment, effort, and perseverance, but the rewards are worth it. With a clear vision of their goals, a growth mindset, and a willingness to learn and grow, individuals can become the best version of themselves and live a fulfilling and meaningful life.

- Embracing Growth Mindset

In recent years, the concept of a growth mindset has gained significant traction in educational and professional settings. Popularized by psychologist Carol Dweck, the growth mindset refers to the belief that intelligence and abilities can be developed through hard work, perseverance, and learning from failures. This stands in contrast to a fixed mindset, which views intelligence and abilities as inherent traits that cannot be changed or improved upon. Embracing a growth mindset can have profound implications for personal growth, academic success, and professional development.

One of the key components of a growth mindset is the willingness to embrace challenges and view them as opportunities for growth. Individuals with a growth mindset understand that overcoming obstacles and setbacks is an essential part of the learning process. Instead of shying away from challenges or giving up at the first sign of difficulty, they approach challenges with a sense of curiosity and determination. This mindset not only fosters resilience and perseverance but also encourages individuals to step out of their comfort zones and push themselves to reach their full potential.

In addition to embracing challenges, cultivating a growth mindset also involves learning from failures and setbacks. Instead of viewing failure as a reflection of their innate abilities, individuals with a growth mindset see it as a temporary setback that provides valuable feedback for improvement. By examining what went wrong, identifying areas for growth, and adjusting their approach accordingly, they can turn failure into a stepping stone for future success. This ability to learn from mistakes and bounce back from failures is a critical skill that can help individuals navigate the complexities of life and achieve their goals.

Furthermore, embracing a growth mindset requires individuals to adopt a positive attitude towards effort and hard work. Rather than viewing talent as the sole determinant of success, individuals with a growth mindset understand that effort and persistence play a crucial role in achieving their goals. This belief in the power of effort and hard work can fuel motivation, build self-confidence, and drive individuals to excel in their endeavors. By setting challenging goals, putting in the necessary effort, and persevering in the face of obstacles, individuals can unlock their full potential and achieve success beyond their wildest dreams.

Another important aspect of embracing a growth mindset is the willingness to seek out feedback and constructive criticism. Instead of viewing feedback as a threat to their self-esteem, individuals with a growth mindset see it as an opportunity for growth and improvement. By soliciting feedback from others, reflecting on their own performance, and using feedback to identify areas for growth, they can continuously evolve and develop their skills. This openness to feedback not only helps individuals identify blind spots and areas for improvement but also fosters a culture of continuous learning and development. By cultivating a willingness to embrace challenges, learn from failures, view effort positively, and seek out feedback, individuals can unlock their full potential and achieve success in all areas of their lives. As psychologist Carol Dweck famously said, "Becoming is better than being. " This mindset encapsulates the essence of a growth mindset – the belief that with effort, perseverance, and a positive attitude, individuals can continuously grow and evolve to reach their full potential. By embracing a growth mindset, individuals can transform their lives, overcome obstacles, and achieve success beyond their wildest dreams.

Chapter 20: Conclusion

- Embracing the Journey of Parenthood

Parenthood is a significant milestone in many people's lives, marking the beginning of a new one filled with joy, challenges, and personal growth. Embracing the journey of parenthood involves navigating the complexities of raising children while also learning more about oneself and the world around them. It requires patience, compassion, and a willingness to adapt to the ever-changing needs of one's children. While the journey of parenthood can be daunting at times, it is also incredibly rewarding and fulfilling, providing parents with a sense of purpose and fulfillment unlike any other.

One of the key aspects of embracing the journey of parenthood is recognizing that there is no "one size fits all" approach to raising children. Every child is unique and will have their own set of needs, personalities, and interests. As such, it is important for parents to approach parenthood with an open mind and a willingness to adapt their parenting style to suit the individual needs of their children. This may involve trying out different parenting techniques, seeking advice from other parents, and constantly reassessing and adjusting one's approach as their children grow and develop.

Another important aspect of embracing the journey of parenthood is practicing self-care and prioritizing one's own well-being. Parenthood can be both physically and emotionally demanding, and it is important for parents to take care of themselves in order to be able to effectively care for their children. This may involve setting aside time for self-care activities, such as exercise, relaxation, or socializing with friends, as well as seeking support from loved ones or professional counselors when needed. By prioritizing their own well-being, parents can ensure that they have the energy and emotional resilience necessary to navigate the challenges of parenthood with grace and compassion.

Communication is also a crucial aspect of embracing the journey of parenthood. Effective communication between parents and their children is essential for building trust, fostering healthy relationships, and promoting positive behavior. Parents should strive to listen to their children's thoughts and feelings, validate their experiences, and communicate openly and honestly with them about important topics. By creating a safe and supportive environment for open communication, parents can strengthen their bond with their children and help them navigate the challenges of growing up with confidence and resilience.

In addition to effective communication, setting boundaries and providing structure for children is another important aspect of embracing the journey of parenthood. Children thrive on routine, consistency, and clear expectations, and it is important for parents to set boundaries and enforce rules in a firm and consistent manner. This helps children feel safe and secure, and provides them with the guidance and structure they need to develop self-discipline and responsibility. By setting appropriate boundaries and providing consistent structure, parents can help their children grow into well-adjusted and confident individuals.

In summary, embracing the journey of parenthood also involves cultivating a sense of gratitude and appreciation for the many blessings that come with raising children. Despite the inevitable challenges and struggles that parenthood may bring, it is important for parents to focus on the positive aspects of their experience and to express gratitude for the joy, love, and fulfillment that their children bring into their lives. By maintaining a mindset of gratitude and appreciation, parents can stay grounded, positive, and resilient in the face of adversity, and can enjoy the journey of parenthood to the fullest. By approaching parenthood with an open mind, practicing self-care, communicating effectively, setting boundaries, and cultivating a sense of gratitude, parents can navigate the challenges of raising children with grace and resilience. Parenthood is a journey filled with ups and downs, but by embracing the process and focusing on the positive aspects of the experience, parents can create lasting memories, build strong relationships with their children, and experience the joy and fulfillment that comes with raising the next generation.

- Committing to Being a Great Parent

Being a great parent is a lifelong commitment that requires dedication, patience, and a willingness to learn and grow. It is not a one-time decision but an ongoing process of making choices that prioritize the well-being and development of your child. As a parent, you have a profound influence on your child's physical, emotional, and cognitive development, and your actions and decisions will shape their beliefs, values, and behaviors for years to come.

One of the key aspects of being a great parent is being present and engaged in your child's life. This means spending quality time with your child, actively listening to their thoughts and feelings, and being responsive to their needs. It also means setting boundaries and guidelines that are appropriate for their age and development and providing a safe and nurturing environment in which they can thrive. By being present and engaged, you can build a strong and trusting relationship with your child that will serve as the foundation for their future relationships and accomplishments.

Another important aspect of being a great parent is being consistent and reliable. Children thrive on consistency and routine, and they rely on their parents to provide a sense of stability and predictability in their lives. By being consistent in your words and actions, you can help your child feel secure and confident in their abilities and decisions. This means following through on your promises, setting clear expectations, and enforcing rules and consequences in a fair and consistent manner. By being reliable, you show your child that they can count on you to be there for them no matter what, which fosters a sense of trust and security in your relationship.

Being a great parent also means being empathetic and understanding towards your child. Parenting can be challenging, and there will inevitably be times when your child's behavior or emotions test your patience and understanding. In these moments, it is important to take a step back and try to see things from your child's perspective. By being empathetic and understanding, you can validate your child's feelings and help them navigate their emotions in a healthy and constructive way. This also means being willing to apologize when you make a mistake or lose your temper, and showing your child that it is okay to admit when you are wrong and to seek forgiveness.

In addition to being present, consistent, and empathetic, being a great parent also means being a positive role model for your child. Children learn by example, and they look to their parents as models for how to behave and interact with the world. By demonstrating kindness, respect, and integrity in your words and actions, you can set a positive example for your child to follow. This includes treating others with kindness and compassion, being respectful and considerate of different perspectives, and standing up for what is right and just. By being a positive role model, you can instill in your child the values and qualities that will help them succeed in life and make a positive impact on their community.

To culminate, being a great parent also means prioritizing your own well-being and self-care. Parenting can be demanding and stressful, and it is important to take care of yourself so that you can be the best parent possible for your child. This means making time for yourself to rest and recharge, seeking support and guidance when needed, and taking care of your physical and emotional health. By prioritizing your own well-being, you can model self-care and resilience for your child, and show them the importance of taking care of themselves in order to be able to care for others. By being present and engaged, consistent and reliable, empathetic and understanding, and a positive role model for your child, you can nurture a strong and loving relationship with your child that will last a lifetime. By prioritizing your own well-being and self-care, you can ensure that you have the energy and resilience needed to be the best parent possible for your child. Remember that parenting is a learning process, and it is okay to make mistakes and seek support and guidance along the way. By committing to being a great parent, you are investing in the future of your child and laying the foundation for a happy, healthy, and successful life.

- Continuing to Learn and Grow as a Parent

Parenting is an ever-evolving journey that requires dedication, patience, and continuous learning. It is a role that comes with no instruction manual, and each child is unique, presenting new challenges and opportunities for growth. As parents, it is crucial to understand that learning and growing in this role is an ongoing process that requires reflection, adaptation, and a willingness to seek out resources and support.

One of the most important aspects of continuing to learn and grow as a parent is to recognize that there is no one-size-fits-all approach to parenting. Each child has their own personality, traits, and needs, and it is essential to adapt your parenting style to meet the individual needs of each of your children. This may require you to be flexible, open-minded, and willing to try new strategies to effectively communicate and connect with your child.

Another key aspect of continuing to learn and grow as a parent is to seek out resources and support. Parenting can be overwhelming at times, and it is important to remember that you are not alone. There are a wealth of resources available, including books, websites, parenting classes, and support groups, that can provide valuable information, guidance, and reassurance. Surrounding yourself with a supportive network of other parents can also be beneficial, as you can share experiences, tips, and advice with one another.

Furthermore, self-reflection is a critical component of continuing to learn and grow as a parent. Take the time to examine your own strengths and weaknesses as a parent, and identify areas where you can improve. Reflect on your interactions with your children, and consider how your actions and words impact their behavior and development. Be open to feedback from others, including your children, and be willing to make changes and adjustments to improve your parenting skills.

In addition, it is important to prioritize your own well-being as a parent. Parenting can be physically, emotionally, and mentally draining, and it is essential to take care of yourself in order to be the best parent you can be. Make time for self-care activities that recharge and rejuvenate you, such as exercise, hobbies, or spending time with friends. Take breaks when needed, and be mindful of your own stress levels and emotional well-being. Remember that taking care of yourself is not selfish - it is essential for your ability to be present and supportive for your children.

Lastly, remember that no parent is perfect, and it is okay to make mistakes. Parenting is a learning process, and we all have moments where we fall short or wish we had handled a situation differently. Instead of dwelling on your mistakes, use them as opportunities for growth and learning. Apologize to your child when necessary, and take steps to make amends and improve your parenting skills. By approaching parenting with a growth mindset and a willingness to learn and adapt, you can continue to grow and evolve as a parent, creating a positive and nurturing environment for your children to thrive.

* 9 7 9 8 2 2 4 7 1 3 0 4 2 *